AF662465

Revised Edition

KNOWLEDGE WHIZZ 3

Kunal Savarkar Seema Chari

Collins

KNOWLEDGE WHIZZ 3

Revised Edition

Kunal Savarkar • Seema Chari

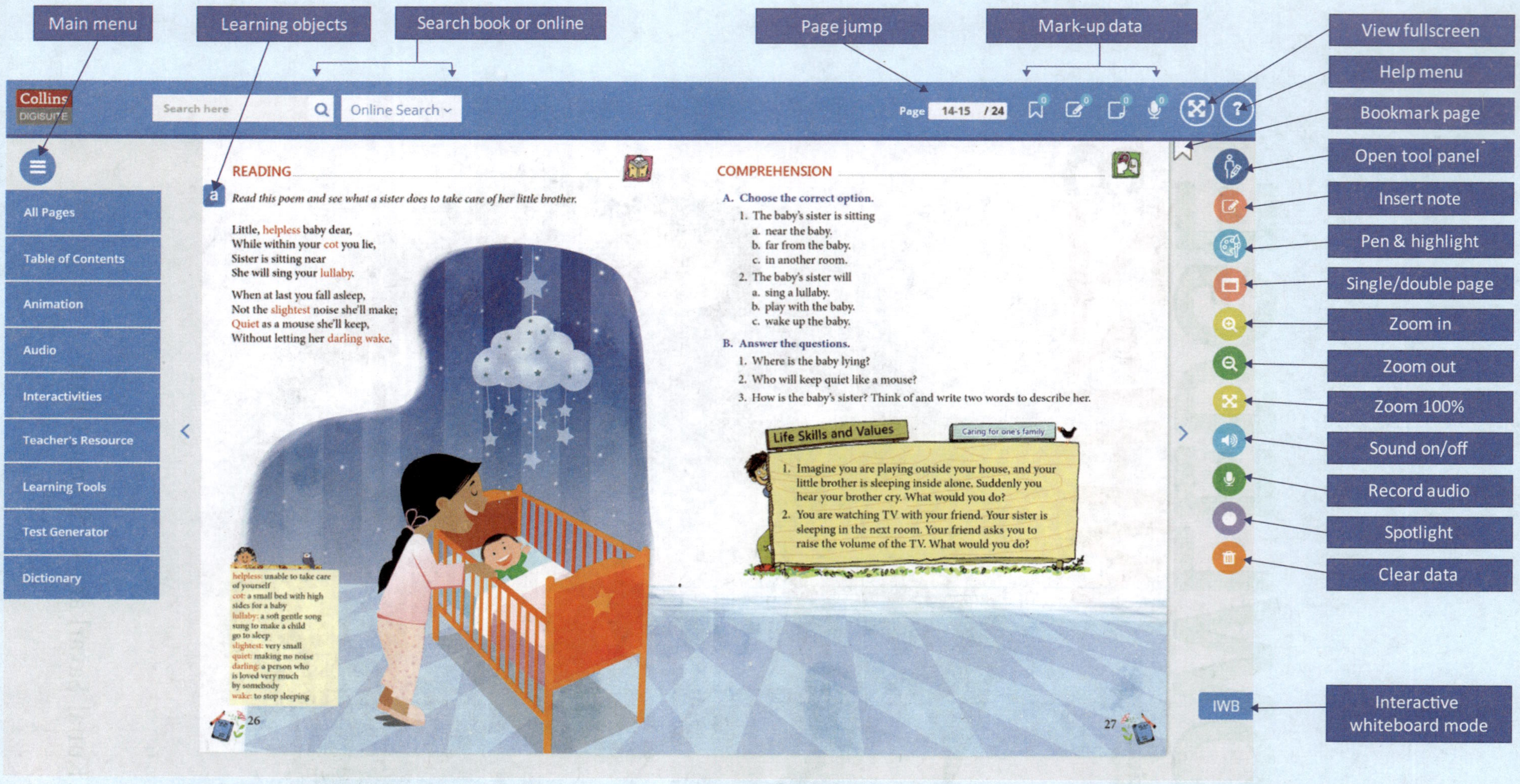

Student + Teacher		Teacher-only	
a animations	ia activities	lp lesson plans	tn teacher's notes
ilt instructor-led tutorials	w worksheets	w worksheets	ak answer keys
g games	v videos		
audio			

Preface

Welcome to ***Knowledge Whizz*** Version 2.0! Our belief that knowledge is for everyone has resonated well across the country, with thousands of school children now using the series, thereby reinforcing our conviction that general knowledge is not the exclusive preserve of a few quizzers. In this multimedia age, knowledge is everywhere, but sourcing, assimilating and recalling it is a skill that can be learned!

Knowledge Whizz, now in its second edition, is a unique series that aims to offer general knowledge covering a wide range of subjects, both curricular as well as extra-curricular, to children from six to thirteen years of age. These are GK books for learning, not quiz books for testing.

Salient features of the series

- Each task comprises at least two kinds of inputs to help children arrive at the answers and acquire knowledge at the same time.
- Tasks cover a wide range of topics presented with a twist. For instance, history includes the story of the automobile, bicycle, cinema, cricket and flight; science includes accidental inventions and discoveries; geography comes alive through associative information and culturally rich chapters. Language and literature cover trivia and etymology, two wonderful learning tools.
- Themes from modern life such as gaming, media, business and finance are extensively explored as well as tidbits about the quirky and the quotidian.
- India-specific content presented beautifully through fun, richly illustrated tasks, designed to whet the curiosity of children and inspire them to explore their beautiful country in all its diversity. New chapters on North East India bring the vibrancy and uniqueness of this relatively lesser known part of India to children everywhere.
- The books do not expect children to be pre-equipped with knowledge but instead reward inquisitiveness by giving them workoutable tasks.
- The artistic and colourful layouts make the presentation more accessible, exciting and alluring whilst facilitating self-learning.
- Special features are an exciting mixed bag of environment education, life skills, values, quick quizzes, cool facts, cool activity, evaluation of multiple intelligences and Higher Order Thinking Skills to make children become well-rounded individuals.
- Brand new features incorporated into Version 2.0 include Aptitudes, aiming to hone and cement specific verbal, visual and logical aptitudes through the common lens of general knowledge, Safety Science, which draws our attention tn the science behind the measures we should take to stay safe wherever we are, and Game, to bring a good dose of fun into learning.

We gratefully acknowledge the contribution of the Xpress Minds Edutainment team, whose inputs have been invaluable for this second edition.

We are certain that this series will open up the world of general knowledge and make learning a fun, instinctive and rewarding process for all.

~ Kunal Savarkar and Seema Chari

In This Book ...

My Time

Read the activity list. Each activity has a colour. Think of the hours you need to do each activity and then colour the right number of slices in the pie chart.

Multiple Intelligence tasks focus on the 8 Intelligences: interpersonal, intrapersonal, bodily kinesthetic, visual-spatial, logical reasoning, verbal-linguistic, naturalistic and musical. Each page explores 5-6 intelligences to encourage learners to learn in their own way and is not to be used for assessment.

Higher Order Thinking Skills (HOTS) pages encourage critical thinking and teach learners to analyse and evaluate information. Cool quizmaster, Kunal Savarkar, helps students become knowledge detectives and skilled quizzers.

Jigsaw Puzzles

A jigsaw puzzle is a game in which we have to fit together pieces with interlocking edges to make a whole picture. Interlocking means pieces have to fit smoothly, like the correct key fits smoothly into its lock.

Here are some easy tips on putting the pieces together.

Cool Activity
Fun activities to learn through doing.

Cool Quiz
Encourages research to find solutions.

Current Affairs
Visit **www.collins.in/knowledgewhizz** for Current Affairs updates and weekly quizzes.

Magic Words and Greetings

A. *Write the following words in the*

Hi!	Wow!	Sorry	Good evening!
Hey!	Yay!	Please	Thank you

Values pages focus on inculcating values, morals, ethics and right attitudes in students through to-do tasks.

Aptitude

Aptitude Tasks are designed to teach children to develop specific skills such as sequencing, classification, analogies and others through rebuses, matching, sorting and pattern activities, with step-by-step tips on how to solve them.

Life Skills pages expose learners to problems in real-life situations to help them learn to take decisions.

Road Rules

People on foot have to follow some rules

COOL FACT

The word 'athletics' comes from either of the two Greek words - athlon meaning prize or athlos meaning competition.

COOL FACT

Factoids linked to the content of the page. The fun element in them will make you say, 'Hey! Cool to know that.'

Green Earth

Green Earth page focuses on environmental issues and imbibes the right attitude towards conservation of environment.

Safety Science

Safety is not just a notion; it is a science, which means it is guided by research, facts and figures. From home to school, public places to controlled environments, we can do a lot to keep ourselves safe. The Safety Science chapters in each book show us how.

Game

Life is a game! Each book in the series has at least one puzzle, maze or strategy-based activity, always with a GK twist, but with the added fell-good incentive of "winning the game".

Quiz Yourself are quick quizzes to assess what the children have learned in the book. The main themes and the cool facts will all form the basis of the Quiz Yourself section, intended as a self-evaluation tool from books 3 to 8.

Detailed Contents

Contents

1 A Tree of Shapes

Do you know these shapes?

The Tree of Shapes has the names of six shapes written in jumbled letters. Put the letters in the right order to spell the name of the shape in the space given below. The starting letter of each shape is coloured in RED.

COOL FACT Any shape with four sides is called a quadrilateral, from the Latin for FOUR (*quattuor*) and SIDE (*latus*). This is a big word, but now, it is so easy to remember.

Magic Words and Greetings

A. *Write the following words in the right columns.*

Hi!	Wow!	Sorry	Good evening!	Hurrah!	Excuse Me
Hey!	Yay!	Please	Thank you	Goodbye!	Goodnight!

1. Magic words	2. Exclamatory words	3. Words of greeting
____________	____________	____________
____________	____________	____________
____________	____________	____________
____________	____________	____________

B. *Look at the situations. Tick the statements that should be said in these situations.*

1. You help an old woman cross the road. The old woman says,
   a. 'Thank you.' ☐
   b. 'Sorry.' ☐
   c. 'Hi!' ☐

2. You visit your neighbour's house in the evening. You greet her by saying,
   a. 'Good evening.' ☐
   b. 'Hey!' ☐
   c. 'Excuse me.' ☐

3. You bump into another child while playing. You would say,
   a. 'Wow!' ☐
   b. 'Sorry!' ☐
   c. 'Good night.' ☐

4. The teacher announces, 'Tomorrow is a holiday.' The children say,
   a. 'Goodbye!' ☐
   b. 'Hurray!' ☐
   c. 'Hi!' ☐

C. *Draw a picture of a situation where any one of the words 'Thank You' or 'Sorry' should be used.*

NATURAL WORLD

2 Fruits, Vegetables or Both

A. Complete the names of these fruits and vegetables. Fill each blank with one letter.

1. ca __ rot 2. st __ a __ be __ r __ 3. a __ p __ e

4. pe __ r 5. p __ mp __ in 6. a __ ric __ t

7. c __ bb __ g __ 8. t __ rn __ p 9. c __ l __ ry

10. gr __ pe 11. p __ ta __ o 12. o __ an __ e

B. Now say the names of the fruits in the fruit basket and the vegetables in the vegetable tray.

1.

fruit basket

2.

vegetable tray

C. Write the names of your favourite fruit and vegetable.

Fruit	Vegetable
______________	______________

COOL FACT In India, two of the most common fruits are banana and mango. They are eaten ripe as fleshy and deliciously sweet fruits. They are also eaten raw in salads and as cooked vegetables in curries and soups.

Count the Fruits

A. *Look at the basket with yellow, red and green apples. Distribute the apples equally amongst the three children and make sure all have apples of each colour! Give an equal number of bananas to each of the three children.*

B. *Now, answer these questions.*

1. How many green, red and yellow apples did each child get? ________
2. How many bananas did each child get? ________
3. How many fruits were left? ________

COOL FACT

When you divide a number by 3, how can you be sure that there will be no remainder? Simple! Just add up the digits. If the total is 3, 6 or 9, it will be perfectly divisible and there will be no remainder.

My Time

This is a chart that looks like a pie. It is called a pie chart. (No. You cannot eat it ☺!) It is divided into 24 slices. A day has 24 hours. Each slice is for one hour of the day.

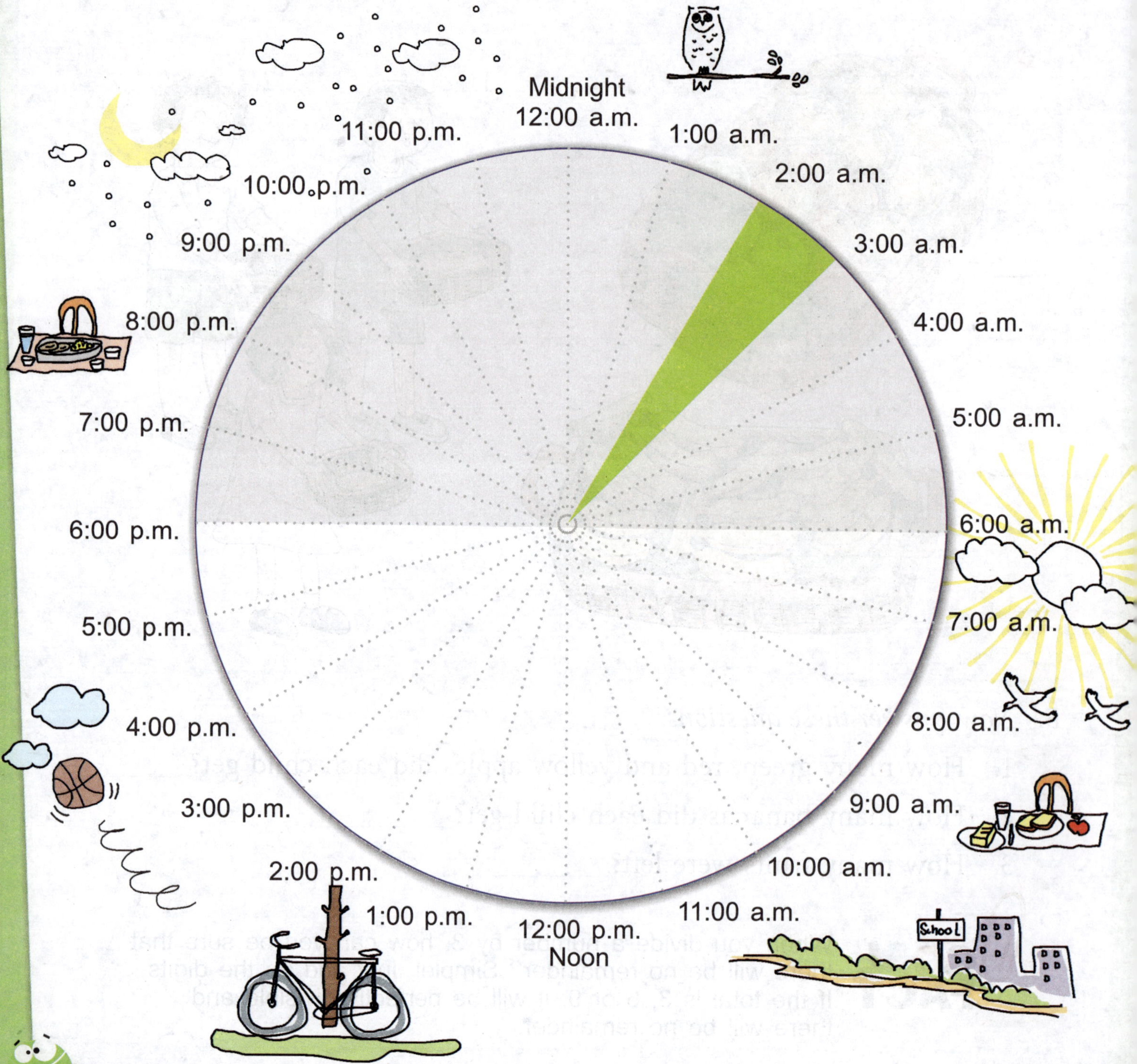

Look at the pictures and read the activities given below them. At what time do you do these activities? How much time do you take to do them? Colour the right number of slices in the pie chart according to the colours given next to each picture.

The time I spend getting ready for school

The time I spend studying in class

The time I spend doing my homework

The time I spend in the school bus coming back home

The time I spend playing or doing fun things

The time I spend having dinner

The time I spend after dinner till bed time

The time I spend sleeping

ART

3

The Colour Wheel

A. *Look at these three colour wheels. Each colour wheel has a number and name.*

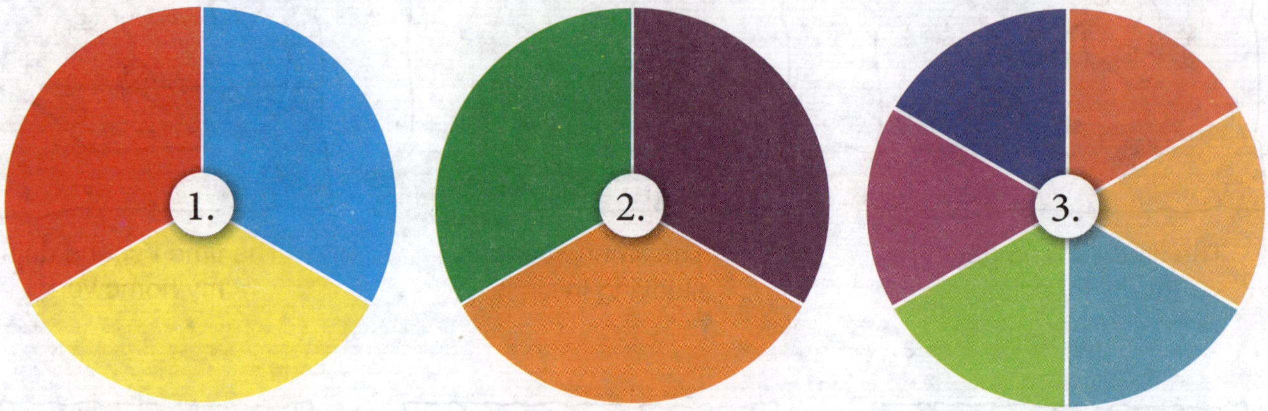

primary colours | secondary colours | tertiary colours

To colour the strawberry with its stalk, choose colours from the numbered colour wheels.

From wheel 1 choose RED for the fruit.
From wheel 2 choose GREEN for the stalk.

B. *Now colour these things by choosing the correct colours from the three wheels and write the number of the colour wheel(s) from which you chose the colour(s), next to the image.*

a.
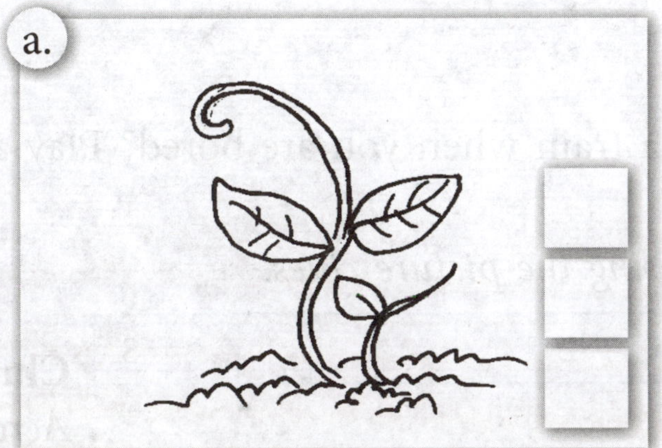
sapling

b.
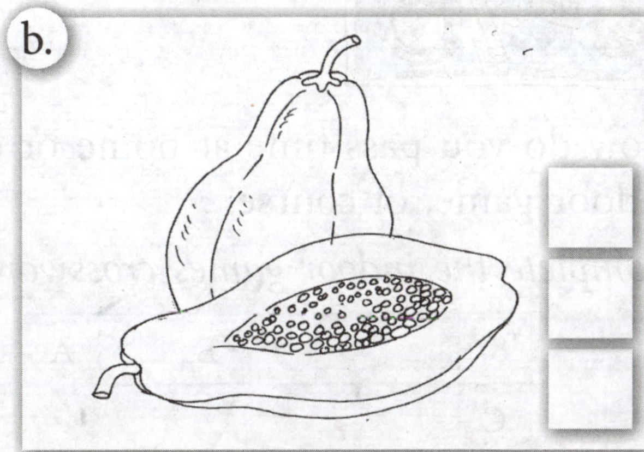
papaya

c.

sky

d.

grapes

e.
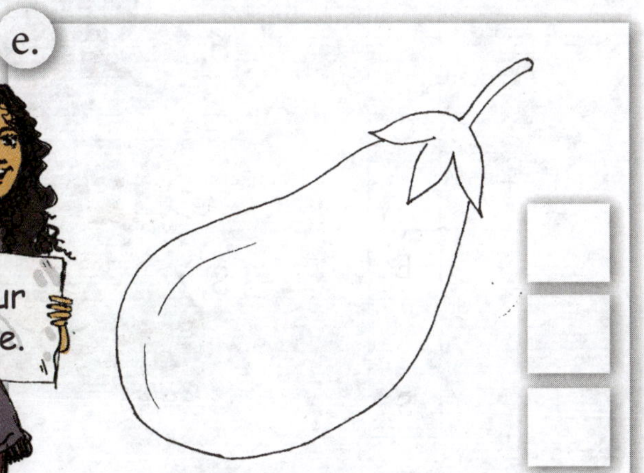
brinjal

f.
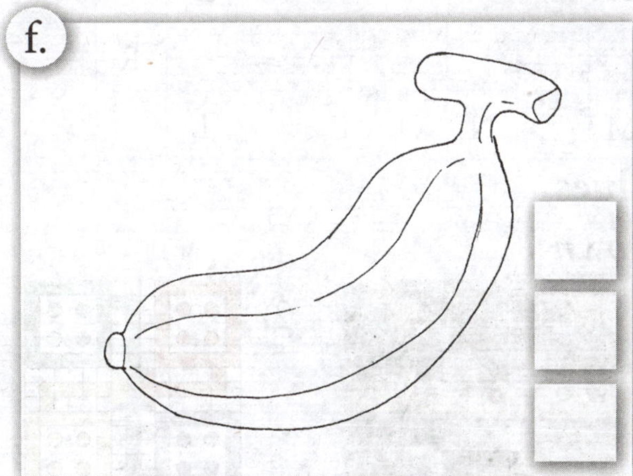
banana

COOL FACT The second colour of the rainbow is indigo. The original blue colour of blue jeans was indigo.

4

Indoor Games

How do you pass time at home or on a train when you are bored? Play an indoor game, of course!

Complete the indoor games crossword using the picture clues.

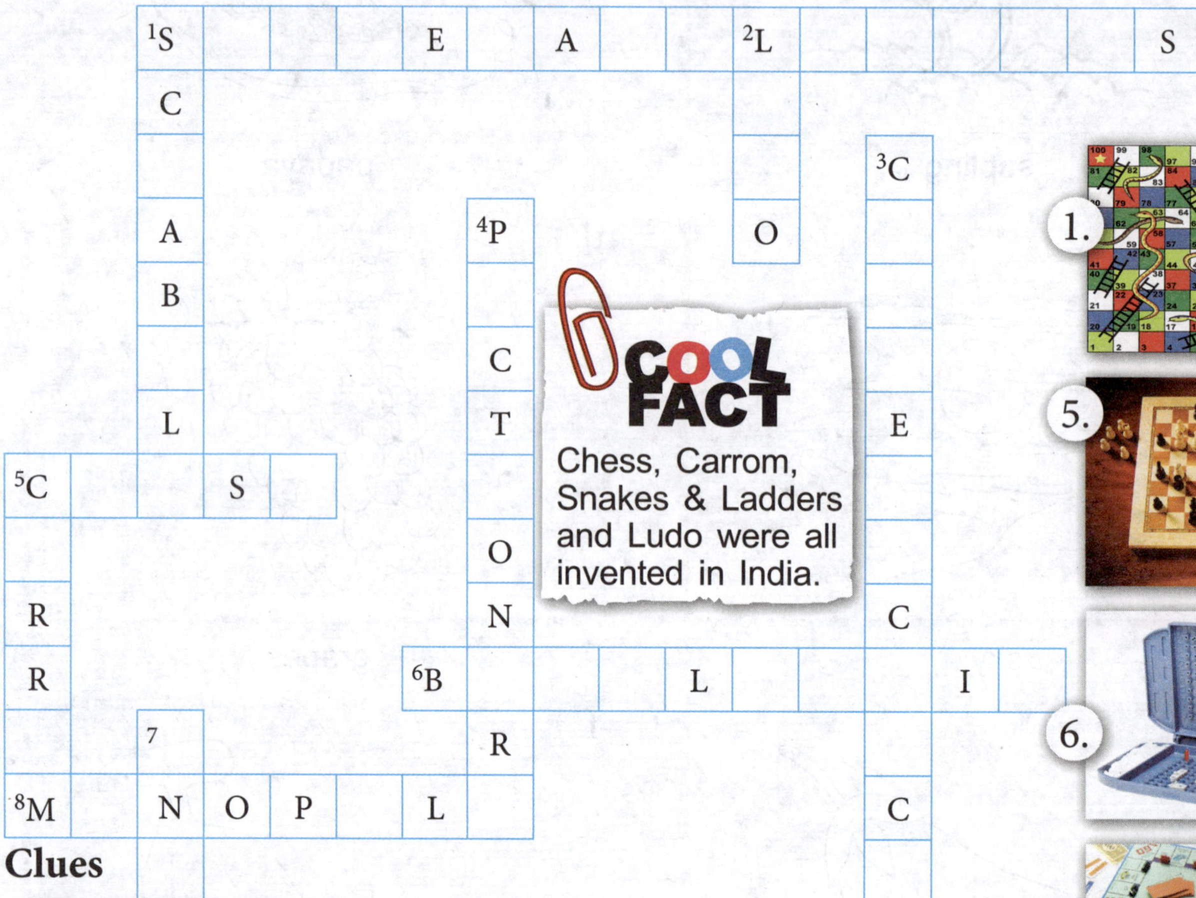

COOL FACT
Chess, Carrom, Snakes & Ladders and Ludo were all invented in India.

Clues

Across

1.
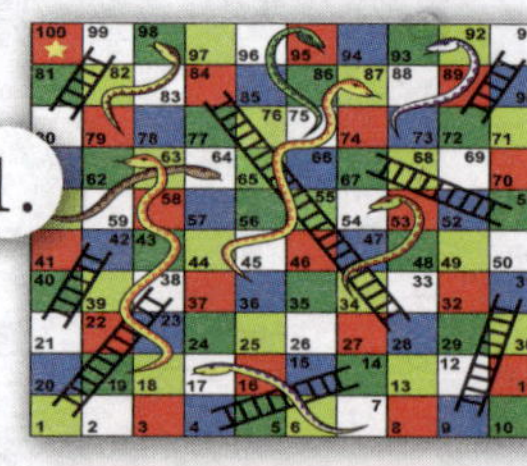

5.

6.
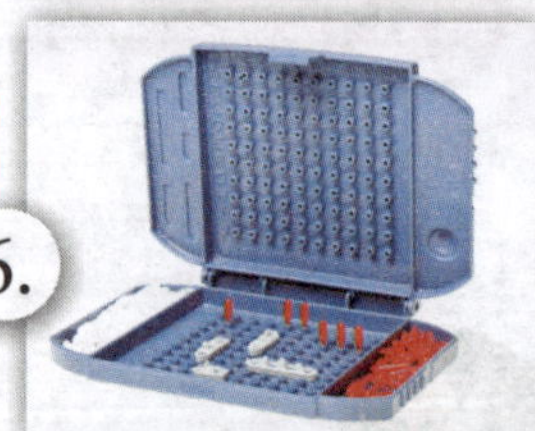

8.

Clues

Down

1.

2.

3.

4.

5.

7.

5

Animal Sounds

A. *Match the pictures of animals with the sounds they make.*

1. 
dolphin

2. 
rooster

3. 
monkey

4. 
owl

5. 
lamb

6. 
pigeon

7. 
elephant

8. 
seal

9. 
wild goose

10. 
hyena

a. chatter
b. click
c. bleat
d. trumpet
e. honk
f. bark
g. crow
h. hoot
i. coo
j. laugh

B. *How many birds are there on this page?* ________

COOL FACT A species of deer called muntjac makes a barking sound when it senses danger. This deer is found in the jungles of India. It is also called the 'barking deer'!

SCIENCE

6

Parts of a Car

A. *Look at the pictures of the parts of a car. From the help box, choose the names of its parts and write them in the given spaces.*

dashboard	headlights	steering wheel	glove compartment
brake	seat belt	fuel indicator	rear-view mirror
wiper	boot	speedometer	accelerator

1. ____________

2. ____________

3. ____________

4. ____________

5. ____________

6. ____________

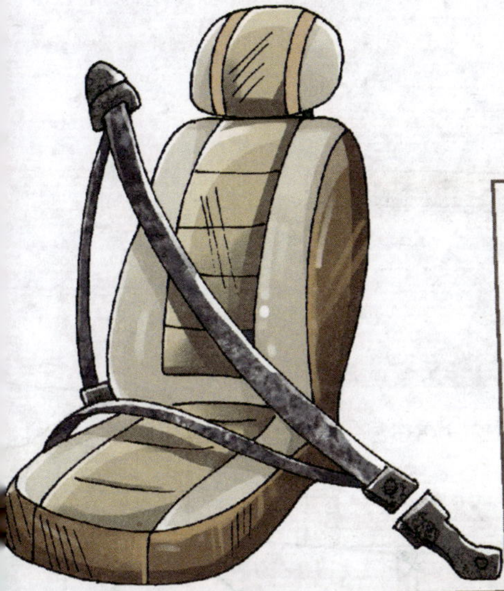

7. ____________

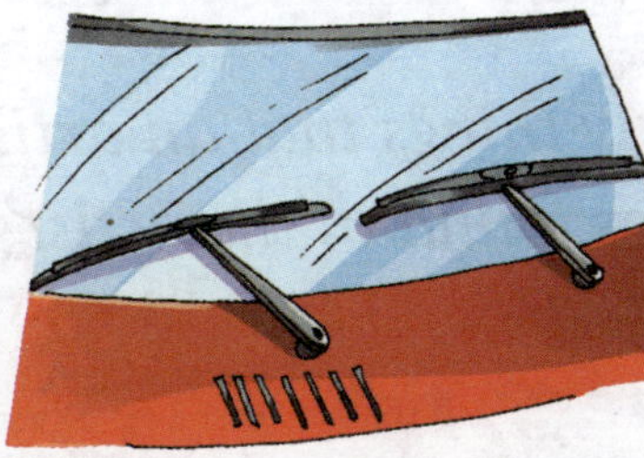

COOL FACT

A convertible is a car that has either a soft roof (made of canvas or cloth) or a hard roof (made of steel or another metal), which can be folded, slid open or shut.

8. ____________

9. ____________

10. ____________

11. ____________

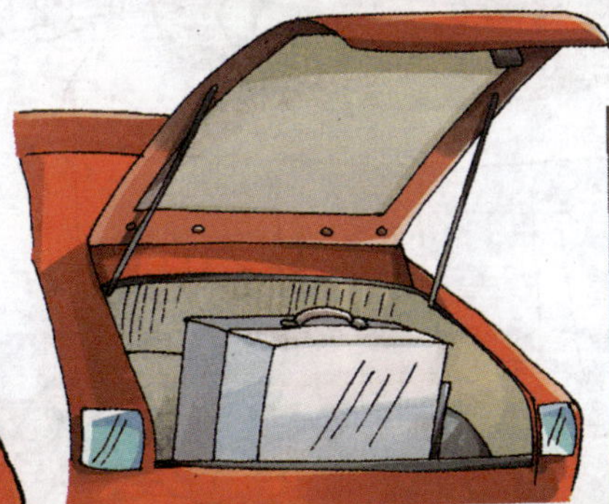

12. ____________

B. *Can you write the name of a part of the car not given in the help box?*

____

ART

7

Artist's Studio

Look at the picture. It has many things that an artist uses. Write the correct number that matches the things found in the artist's studio next to each word in the list.

a. easel ☐

b. palette ☐

c. brush ☐

d. paints ☐

e. still life ☐

f. water mug ☐

g. canvas ☐

h. apron ☐

i. rag ☐

j. model ☐

COOL FACT You do not always need a paintbrush to paint. You can use rags, fingers, vegetables, cotton, crushed paper, spray guns, toothbrushes and many other things. Can you think of some more?

ENTERTAINMENT

8

Pets from Comics

A. *Match these famous pet owners from storybooks with their pets. A picture clue has been given. Choose their names from the options in the help box.*

Dino Mouse Hedwig Snowy Dinah

1. Tintin	2. Harry Potter	3. Judy Moody	4. Alice in Wonderland	5. Fred Flintstone

________	________	________	________	________

B. *Now draw your favourite storybook pet and owner.*

COOL FACT

Spike, Butch and Bulldog are three names for the same cat-hating and mouse-loving dog in the Tom and Jerry animated series.

Jigsaw Puzzles

A jigsaw puzzle is a game in which we have to fit together pieces with interlocking edges to make a whole picture. Interlocking means pieces have to fit smoothly, like the correct key fits smoothly into its lock.

Here are some easy tips on putting the pieces together.

1. First of all, look for the four corner pieces. They will have two straight sides.
2. Second, find the side pieces. All of them have at least one straight side.
3. Look for picture details like grass, tip of star or dress, flower petal edge, animal tail, etc.
4. Put together pieces that make up parts of the picture and start filling from outside to inside.
5. Repeat this for different chunks of the picture.
6. Look at piece patterns and note which way the piece is facing. Left or right? Up or down? How big is the stub or slot? Do the sizes match?
7. Step back and admire your beautiful jigsaw puzzle!

AROUND THE WORLD

9

Special Vehicles

Read my description and look at my picture. What am I? Choose the correct options from the help box and fill in the blanks.

1.

I am red in colour and make a lot of noise, while on the road, with my siren and my bell. What am I?

____

2.

I am on hospital duty and I flash a red light and sound a siren to ask the traffic to give me right of way. What am I?

____

3.

I have blue and red lights on my head. I help in catching thieves and those who break the law. What am I?

____

4.

I have a strong body which helps in moving earth, rocks and stones. I can demolish buildings too. What am I?

____

5.

I am red in colour. I carry sacks of letters and parcels. What am I?

____

6.

I can lift heavy things and place them wherever needed. What am I?

____

7.

I move heavy things on railway tracks. What am I?

____

crane
ambulance
goods train
police car
fire engine
bulldozer
postal van

COOL FACT The word 'ambulance' is always written backwards so that other drivers are able to read it easily in their rear-view mirrors and give it right of way.

Identifying Patterns

How do you know that a particular piece would fit in a particular place in a jigsaw puzzle? Easy! You actually place it there. If it fits, it will sit there perfectly! But what of puzzles of the mind? These are puzzles which have 'missing pieces' that you have to 'fit' to complete the picture. Detectives use clues to 'fit' pieces of a puzzle and understand how a crime was committed.

Look at the following string of pictures. Such a string is called a 'sequence', which means that each piece in the string comes in an order before or after another.

In this sequence, one piece is left blank and you have to fill it.
Let's see how you would do it.

1.

In this sequence, each little bug is the same. But each bug has a different number of dots on its back. Look closely at the dots. The first bug has 2 dots. The second has 3 dots. The third has 4 dots. The fifth has 6 dots. How many dots do you think the fourth one should have?

Now complete these sequences to solve the puzzles. Explain why you wrote that answer.

2.

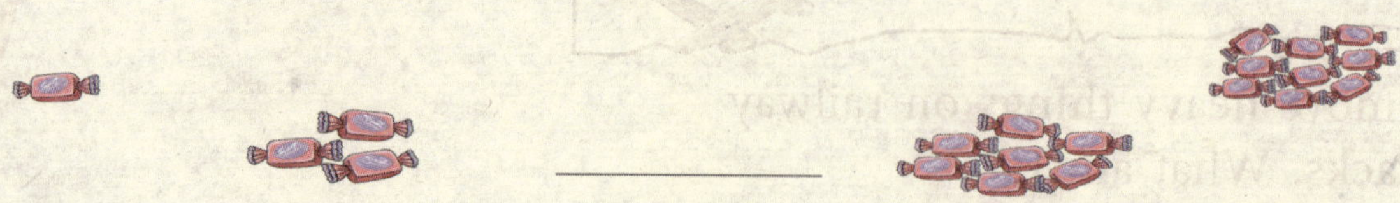

3.

___ *A b* ___ ___ *C d D*

4. 

5. 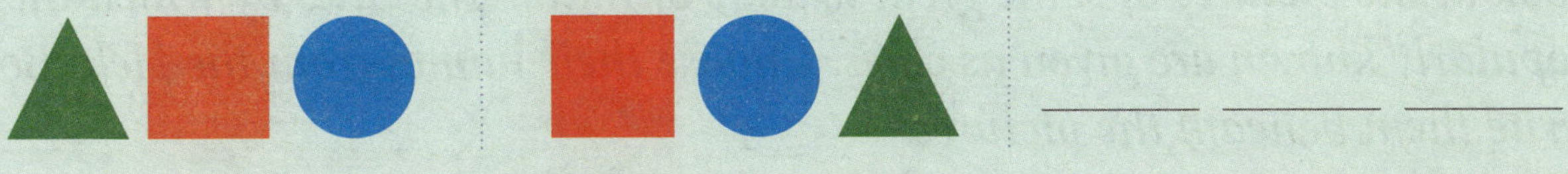

6. *u v w* *u v w* ___ ___ ___

7. 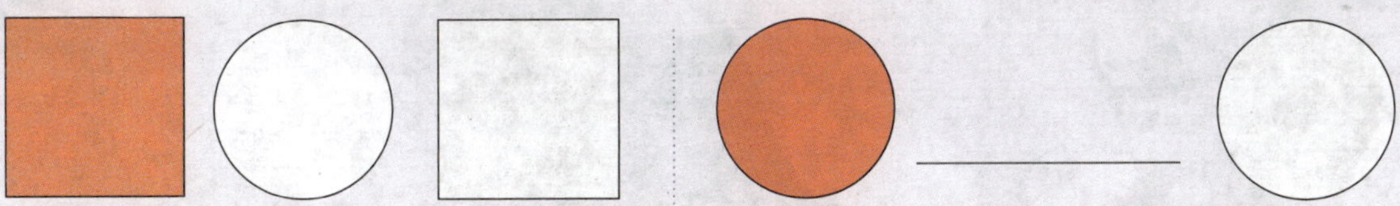

8. Lm, ___ ___, ___ ___, Rs, Tu

9. def, ___ ___ ___, fgh, ghi, ___ ___ ___

10. 1 3, 2 4, ___ ___, 4 6, ___ ___, 6 8

11. 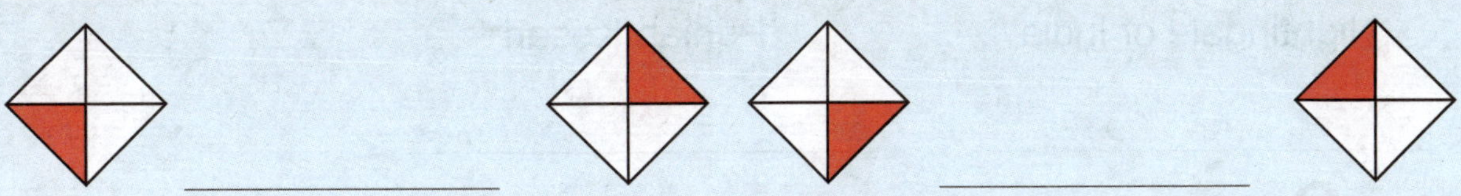

12. 2 3 4, ___ ___ ___, 6 9 12, ___ ___ ___

10 Popular Names for Our Leaders

Look at the pictures of some great leaders of India. The titles by which they are popularly known are given as clues. Choose their names from the Help Box and write them beneath the pictures.

1.

Father of the Nation

____

2.

Grand Old Man of India

____

3.

Iron Man

____

4.

Nightingale of India

____

5.

Punjab Kesari

____

Dadabhai Naoroji
Lala Lajpat Rai
Sardar Vallabhbhai Patel
Sarojini Naidu
Mahatma Gandhi

COOL FACT Famous personalities are often given nicknames connected to their style or achievements. Two examples are Master-Blaster (Sachin Tendulkar) and the Lady with the Lamp (Florence Nightingale). Can you think of any others?

INDIA

11

Our National Anthem

A. *How well do you really know our National Anthem? Fill in the blanks and complete it. Time yourself and see how fast you can complete it!*

Jana-gana- 1. ____________ -adhinayaka, jaya he,

Bharata-bhagya- 2. ____________ .

Punjab-Sindh- 3. ____________ -Maratha,

4. ____________ -Utkala-Banga,

Vindhya-Himachala- 5. ____________ -Ganga
Uchchala-Jaladhi-taranga.

Tava shubha name 6. ____________ ,
Tava shubha asisa 7. ____________ ,

Gahe tava jaya 8. ____________ ,

Jana-gana- 9. ____________ -dayaka jaya he
Bharata- 10. ____________ -vidhata.

Jaya he, jaya he, jaya he,
Jaya jaya jaya, jaya he!

COOL FACT

Rabindranath Tagore is the only poet to have composed the national anthems of two countries: India and Bangladesh. The Sri Lankan National Anthem is also based on the translation of a Bengali song written by Tagore.

Gujarat Dravida mana mage Yamuna jage mangala bhagya gatha vidhata

B. *Write T for True and F for False for these statements about the national anthem.*

1. The national anthem was written by Rabindranath Tagore in Hindi. ☐
2. The Indian national anthem is to be sung in 52 seconds. ☐
3. One can sit and talk while the national anthem is being played. ☐

SCIENCE

12

All Kinds of Plants

Look at this lovely garden. There are shrubs, trees, herbs and climbers growing here. Write their names in the correct columns.

Trees	Shrubs	Climbers	Herbs

COOL FACT

Creepers and climbers look quite similar but they are different. While creepers grow along the ground, climbers grow upwards, along or around a support.

Rebus

Some of us find words fun. Some find pictures fun. Some find sounds fun. But think how much more fun one can have if we could mix all three!

In fact, using pictures or sounds is a great way to learn. They help us remember things in a more complete way.

Combining letters with sounds also helps us to improve our spelling (how to write words) and pronunciation (how to say words). Adding and subtracting letters to get new words makes us think of how to say or write the new words too.

Here is an example:

 +  − ST + C = 

ice cream

A. *Now try these:*

1.  +  =  ______________

2.  +  =  ______________

3. 

− A + 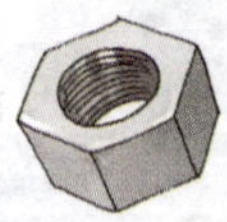 =  ______________

4.  − T +  =  ______________

5.  − P + T +  =  ______________

B. *Rebuses work with places too. Solve these to get the names of some world cities. One has been done for you.*

1.  – H +  = Amsterdam

   hamster dam

2. SYD +  = ____________

3.  – S +  = ____________

4. HONG +  –  = ____________

5.  – H + R = ____________

C. *You can make and solve rebuses about events, books, people and movies too! Try these.*

1. BOSTON +  +  = ____________

2.  +  = ____________

3.  – E +  + MOVEMENT = ____________

4.  – I + R +  = ____________

5.  +  = ____________

COOL FACT Did you enjoy solving these word sums? They are called rebuses and they use pictures to represent words.

SPORTS

13 The Athletics Stadium

A. *Match the pictures with the names of the athletic events given below.*

1.

2.

3.

4.

5.

6.

7.

8.

9.

10.

a. 100 m
b. shot-put
c. hurdles
d. discus throw
e. hammer throw
f. javelin throw
g. pole vault
h. high jump
i. long jump
j. relay

B. *Sort the games given above into these three groups.*

Running events	Jumping events	Throwing events
________	________	________
________	________	________
________	________	________
________	________	________
________	________	________

COOL FACT

The word 'athletics' comes from either of the two words *athlon* meaning 'prize' and *athlos* meaning 'competition'.

Save, Don't Waste!

Here are some things you do in your daily lives. For each of these situations, both answers are correct. Tick (✓) the answer that helps the environment.

1. If you missed school and you copied all the work that was done in your notebook,
   a. you would learn the lesson better since you wrote the notes by yourself. ☐
   b. you would save electricity and extra paper by not photocopying. ☐

2. You used the carpool to go to school so
   a. there were fewer cars on the road and therefore less pollution. ☐
   b. you could make friends with other children in the carpool. ☐

3. If you use your elder brother or sister's old books,
   a. your elder brother/sister would have to maintain things in good condition. ☐
   b. you save trees from being cut. ☐

4. If you cleaned your bicycle with a wet piece of cloth and a small bucket of water,
   a. you will not waste water, which would happen if you used a hose. ☐
   b. your bicycle will look nice and pretty. ☐

5. If you washed your face with soap, using a mugful of water without leaving the tap open,
   a. you would not waste water due to an open tap. ☐
   b. your soap would not get over quickly. ☐

6. If you placed your desk and chair near the open windows during a sunny day,
   a. there would be more space to play in the room. ☐
   b. you would save energy because you would not need to switch on an electric light. ☐

AROUND THE WORLD

14

Let's Visit Australia

A. *Match the columns showing some easy facts about Australia.*

1. Capital	a. English
2. Biggest city	b. Great Barrier Reef
3. Currency	c. Australian dollar
4. Official language	d. Canberra
5. Meaning of Australia	e. Sydney
6. Island state	f. aboriginals
7. World's largest coral reef	g. Southern Land
8. Native people of Australia	h. Tasmania

B. Australia has a group of strange but interesting animals called marsupials that carry their babies in a pouch on their bodies.

Make words using the picture clues and add or subtract letters as required to get the names of few marsupials. One has been done for you.

1.  − T + $\begin{array}{r} 110 \\ +15 \\ \hline 125 \\ \hline \end{array}$ = 

possum

2.  − C + K + A = 

____

3.  − C + K +  − TE + 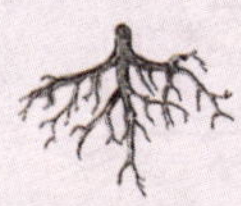 − T = 

____

4. TAS +  − BAT + IAN +  = 

____

COOL FACT Australia is in the southern hemisphere, so it has summer in December and winter in June.

At the Restaurant

Look at the picture of a restaurant. Write the correct letter that matches the things found in the restaurant next to each word in the list below.

1. Table ☐
2. Chair ☐
3. Glass for water ☐
4. High chair ☐
5. Plate ☐
6. Napkin ☐
7. Fork ☐
8. Knife ☐
9. Soup bowl with spoon ☐
10. Salt and pepper shakers ☐
11. Restroom door ☐
12. Menu card ☐
13. Kitchen door ☐
14. Billing counter ☐
15. Waiter ☐

Kitchen
k.
n.
o.
l.
b.
i.
j.
m.
d.
h.
g.

LOGICAL REASONING

15 Length of Time

Read these activities. The time when each activity started is given, along with how long it took to be completed. In the blank space, write at what time the activity got over. Also draw the hour and minute hands in the blank clock. The first one has been done for you.

1. The cake was put in the oven at three-fifteen in the afternoon and took forty-five minutes to bake. The cake was baked at 4:00 p.m.

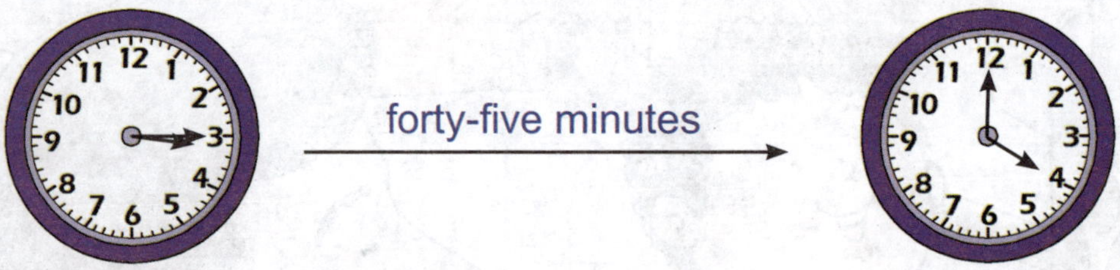

3:15 p.m. 4:00 p.m.

2. The cricket practice started at four-forty-five in the afternoon and lasted two and a half hours. ____________________

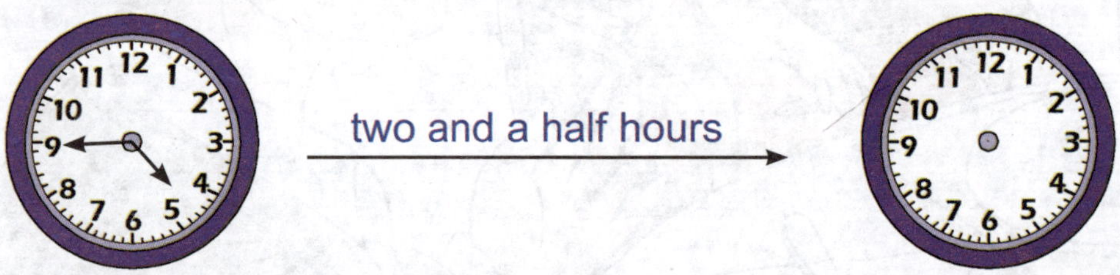

4:45 p.m. ____________

3. The train left the station at ten-fifty in the morning and reached its destination after eight hours. ____________________

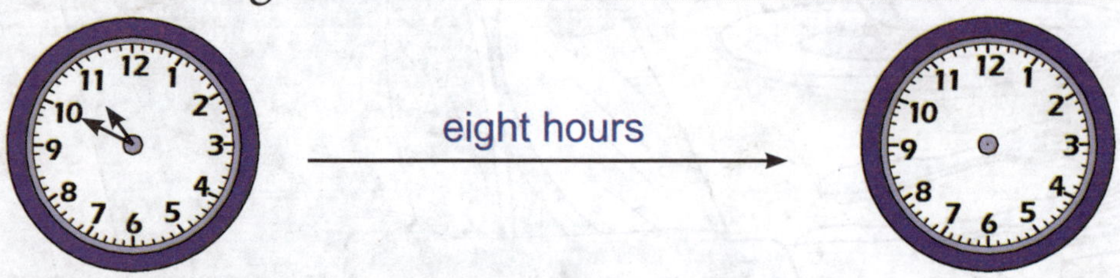

10:50 a.m. ____________

COOL FACT Cricket is played in three formats based on how long the match is played: T20, which is twenty overs per team; One-Day International, which is fifty overs per team; and the Test Match, which could go up to 5 days.

4. The swimming race started at ten past ten in the morning and went on for twenty minutes. ______________________

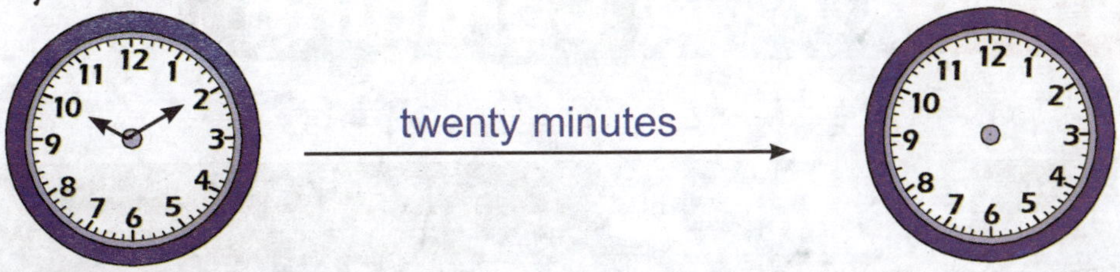

10:10 a.m.

____

5. The break in school begins at twelve-twenty-five and it ends after twenty-five minutes. ______________________

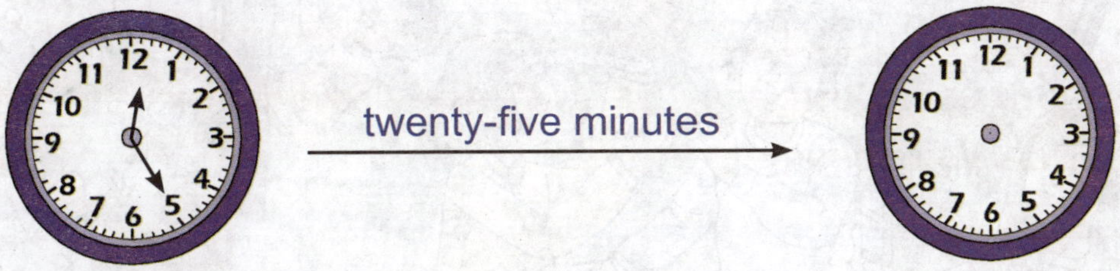

12:25 p.m.

____

6. Rita started to do her homework at three-forty in the afternoon and finished after two hours and forty minutes. ______________

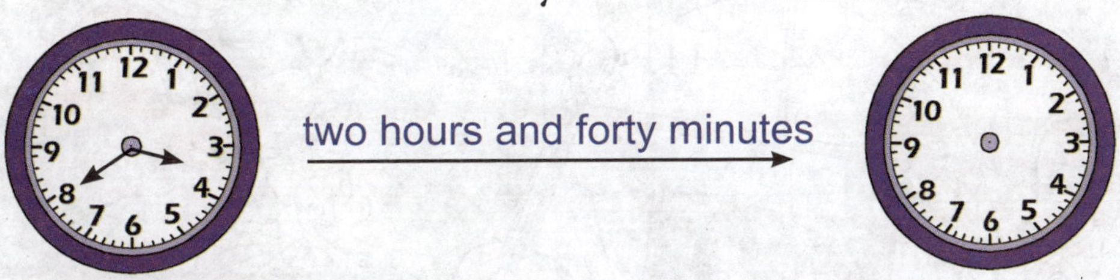

3:40 p.m.

____

7. The football game started at 2 o' clock in the afternoon and lasted for ninety minutes. ______________________

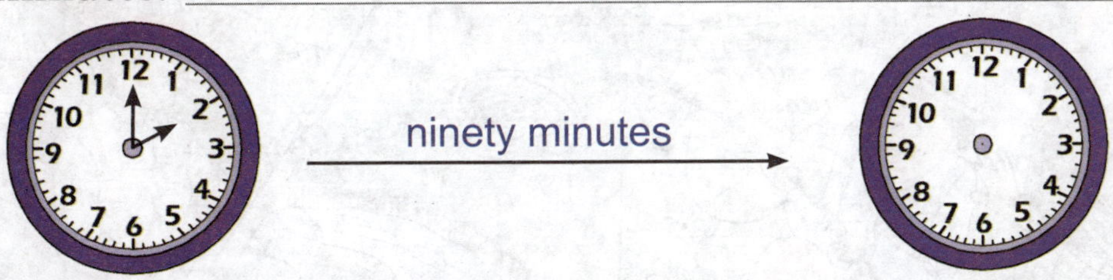

2:00 p.m.

____

8. Seema leaves her house at seven-twenty to go to the bus stop and reaches school after fifty minutes. ______________

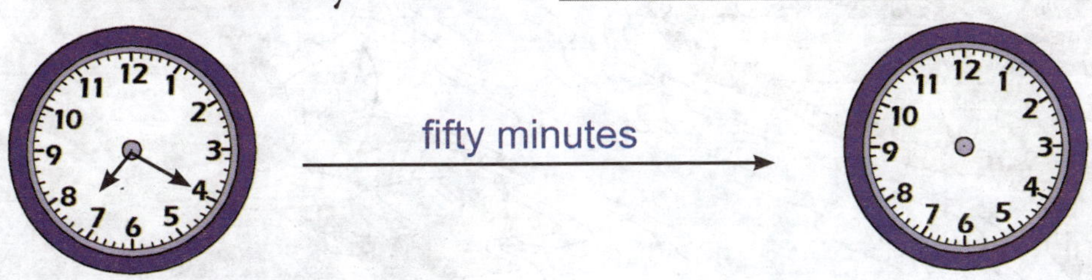

7:20 a.m.

____

We're Going Camping

Play this game in teams of four or more persons. Make 24 little chits with these 24 letters. Each team will have one person who will choose a letter and describe something in the campsite starting with that letter. You are not allowed to say the word. You can only give clues by describing it. Write the words in the space given below. The team that finishes all its letters first and has written at least half of the words shown in the picture wins!

S	L	S	M	B	C	W	T	M	T	L	C
F	G	F	R	R	B	S	R	P	C	B	B

1. Squirrel
2. ______
3. ______
4. ______
5. ______
6. ______
7. ______
8. ______
9. ______
10. ______
11. ______
12. ______
13. ______
14. ______
15. ______
16. ______
17. ______
18. ______
19. ______
20. ______
21. ______
22. ______
23. ______
24. ______

SPORTS

16

Indian Olympic Champs

Here are some Indian sportspeople who have won medals at the Olympic Games. Each champion below is holding a gold, silver or a bronze medal.

A. *Look at the colour of the medal carefully and complete the sentence about each champion. One has been done for you.*

1. PV Sindhu won the ___silver___ medal in badminton in 2016.

2. Rajyavardhan Rathore won the ________ medal in shooting in 2004.

3. Karnam Malleswari won the ________ medal in weightlifting in 2000.

4. Abhinav Bindra won the ________ medal in shooting in 2008.

5. Leander Paes won the ________ medal in tennis in 1996.

6. Vijender Singh won the ________ medal in boxing in 2008.

COOL FACT

The first person to win medals for India in the Olympic Games was Norman Pritchard. He won two silver medals in the Paris Games of 1900. In 1952, at the Helsinki Olympics, KD Jadhav won a bronze in wrestling.

7. Sushil Kumar won the _________ medal in wrestling in 2008.

8. Sakshi Malik won the _________ medal in wrestling in 2016.

B. *India's sports champions won a record 6 medals at the 2012 Olympic Games. Match them with their pictures. The logos will help you.*

1. Saina Nehwal won a bronze in	☐
2. Yogeshwar Dutt won a bronze in	☐
3. Sushil Kumar won a silver in	☐
4. Gagan Narang won a bronze in	☐
5. Vijay Kumar won a silver in	☐
6. Mary Kom won a bronze in	☐

a.

shooting

b.

boxing

c.

badminton

d.

wrestling

e.

shooting

f.

wrestling

Useful Plants

A. *Look at these pictures and their names. All of these things come from plants. Put them into two groups: things that we can eat (edible) and things that we cannot eat (inedible).*

strawberry

paper

corn

coir mat

jasmine perfume

aloe vera gel

mustard

pineapple

rice

sugarcane

rubber

gunny sack

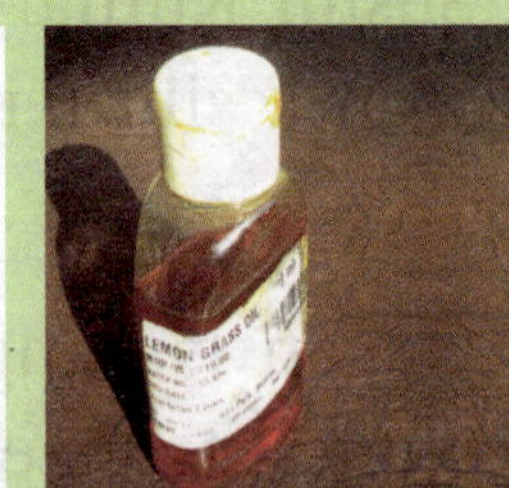
lemongrass oil

groundnut

cotton dress

wheat

pencil

broom

Now write the names in the correct columns.

Things that we can eat (edible)	Things that we cannot eat (inedible)

B. *Write the names of two more edible things and two more inedible things that we get from plants here.*

Edible Things

1. ______________________________

2. ______________________________

Inedible Things

1. ______________________________

2. ______________________________

COOL FACT One of the most useful plants found is the banana plant. Its stem, flowers and fruits are eaten, and its large leaves are used as traditional use-and-throw plates.

TRIVIA

17

Name the Months

Read these sentences to name the months of the year.

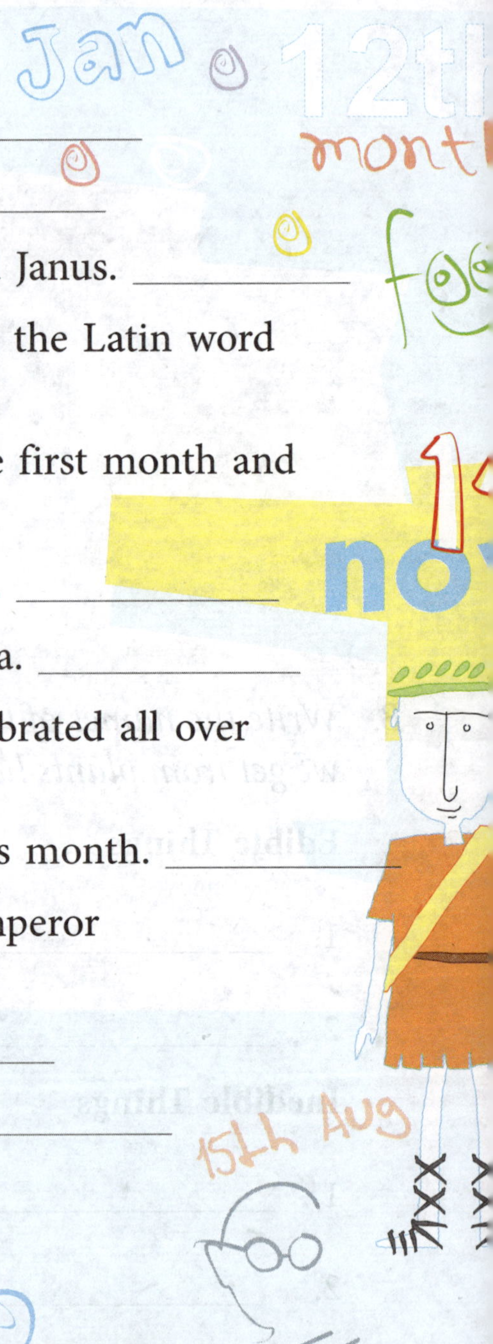

1. The month with the least number of days. ____________
2. The first of this month is All Fools Day. ____________
3. This month is named after a two-faced god called Janus. ____________
4. This is the ninth month but its name comes from the Latin word for seven. ____________
5. According to the early Roman calendar, it was the first month and was called Martius. ____________
6. The Father of the Nation was born in this month. ____________
7. Children's Day is celebrated in this month in India. ____________
8. This month is famous for Labour Day that is celebrated all over the world. ____________
9. India got its independence from the British in this month. ____________
10. This month is named after the famous Roman emperor Julius Caesar. ____________
11. Christmas is celebrated in this month. ____________
12. The longest day of the year is in this month. ____________

COOL FACT

Here is a simple poem to help you remember which month has how many days:

Thirty days has September;
April, June and November;
February has twenty-eight alone;
And all the rest have thirty-one!

SCIENCE

18

Sources of Light

The Sun is a source of natural light. There are other sources of light too.

Fill in the blanks with the names of other sources of light using the labelled pictures on the side.

1. If a small thing has fallen and rolled under a piece of furniture, you can look for it by switching on a ______________.
2. Plants grow when they have water, good soil, air and ______________.
3. When a cricket match is played at night, the ______________ are switched on.
4. When you go camping in the hills and want to warm yourself and keep wild animals away, you light a ______________.
5. If there is no electricity, you can have dinner using light from a ______________, which is made of wax.
6. For Diwali, earthen oil lamps called ______________ are lighted.
7. ______________ beams are used to produce sharp points or lines of light in the sky, like in coloured fountains, on buildings or just a fancy light display for a show or even sports events.
8. The most advanced and long-lasting source of light for homes and commercial spaces is the ______________, which saves energy, because unlike a normal bulb, it does not produce heat.

floodlights

laser

diyas

sunlight

torch

fire

candle

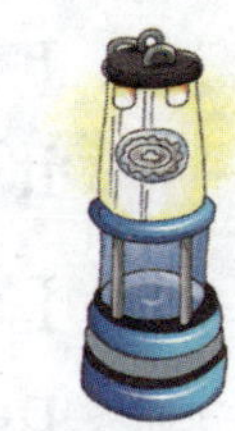

LED bulb

COOL FACT

Any light that flashes on and off, such as on ambulances, on the tails of aeroplanes, on the tops of TV and radio towers or lighthouses, is called a strobe.

Eating Out

You are in a restaurant with your family. At each of these times, what would you do? Tick (✓) the correct answer.

1. You have reached the restaurant. What would you do first?

   a. We would find a table and sit down. ☐

   b. I would walk all around the restaurant. ☐

2. You have placed your order. It will take fifteen minutes to arrive. What would you do to pass time?

   a. My brother/sister and I would play games on a smartphone. ☐

   b. We would chat softly while waiting. ☐

3. The restaurant has placed a fork, knife, spoon, plate, bowl and napkin on each person's place mat. How would you use them?

   a. I would play drums using the cutlery and bowl to pass time. ☐

   b. I would spread the napkin on my lap and use the cutlery with care. ☐

4. The waiter serves your food. What would you do?

   a. I would eat neatly, even if it takes a bit longer to eat. ☐

   b. I would eat as quickly as possible, even if I make a mess. ☐

5. You have had your meal and are now waiting for the dessert. What would you do while you wait?

a. I would talk to my parents in a low voice as we wait. ☐

b. I would use the salt, pepper and pickles to invent new dishes. ☐

6. You need to go to the restroom. What would you do?

a. I would ask the waiter softly. ☐

b. I would ask the waiter loudly, so that others also get to know. ☐

7. You have spilled some ice cream on your chin and dress. What would you do?

a. I would wipe off the ice cream with my sleeve. ☐

b. I would wipe off the ice cream with a napkin. ☐

8. Your ice cream is now finished. What would you do?

a. I would get up and leave quietly. ☐

b. I would race with my brother/sister to the exit. ☐

LANGUAGE AND LITERATURE

19

Comparing Colours

If you are a good child, your mother or teacher might say, 'You are as good as gold.' This is called a simile (si-mi-lee).

Use the pictures as clues and complete the similes. All of them are about colours.

a.

b.

c.

d.

e.

1. as red as a __________
2. as white as __________
3. as grey as the __________
4. as black as __________
5. as black as the __________
6. as pink as a __________
7. as blue as the __________

f.

g.

h. mud

i. grass

j. tangerine

8. as blue as the ______________
9. as yellow as a ______________
10. as green as ______________
11. as golden as ______________
12. as brown as ______________
13. as white as a ______________
14. as orange as a ______________

k. honey

l. daffodil

n. sea

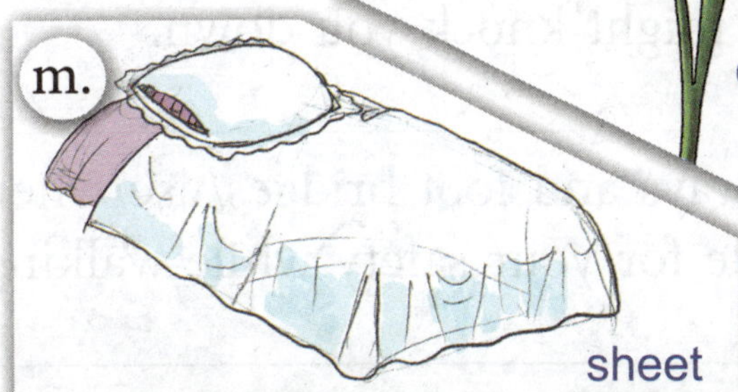
m. sheet

These similes are very common. Try making up some of your own, like this example:

- as green as <u>mint chutney</u>
- as red as ______
- as blue as ______
- as white as ______
- as black as ______
- as brown as ______
- as yellow as ______
- as orange as ______
- as violet as ______

Road Rules

Even when you walk, you must follow road rules.

Here are eight rules given in jumbled sentences. Put the words in the correct order and use capital letters in the correct place. The sentences in the brackets are the clues.

1. down from a/wait for people to get/bus or train. (You can get in after that.)

   ____

2. do not/the road/play on. (You can get run over by passing vehicles.)

   ____

3. the footpath wherever/walk on/possible. (The main road is supposed to be for traffic.)

   ____

4. a zebra crossing/cross only at. (People should cross the road there.)

   ____

5. adult's hand while/crossing the road/hold an. (Running across a road all by yourself is dangerous.)

   ____

6. the direction/always walk facing/of traffic. (Traffic coming from behind you might knock you down.

   ____

7. subways and foot bridges/use/wherever available. (These are specially made for your safety while walking across busy roads.)

   ____

8. when the/lights up you/green man/can cross. (This means that traffic has to wait for people to walk across.)

   ____

COOL FACT

In big cities all over the world, there are zones where vehicles are not allowed. In India too, in some big cities, traffic-free zones are being made for people to walk and play in. Walking is much healthier and fun than travelling or moving in a vehicle!

ENTERTAINMENT

20

Mobile Games

Use the picture and word clues to make the names of eight mobile games that people love to play. The first one has been done for you.

1.  +  + JOYRIDE = JETPACK JOYRIDE

JET PACK

2.  +  = ____________

3.  +  = ____________

4. WHERE'S MY +  = ____________

5. 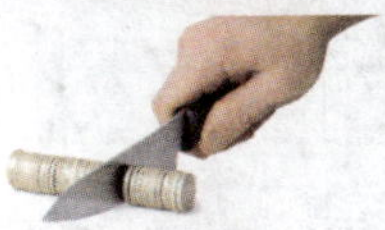 + THE +  = ____________

6.  +  = ____________

7.  +  = ____________

8.  +  + SAGA = ____________

COOL FACT The oldest mobile phone game is Tetris, invented by a Russian designer named Alexey Pajitnov, who combined the Greek word *Tetra* (meaning four) with tennis (his favourite game) and coined this word.

SAFETY SCIENCE

21 Safety in School

You spend about thirty hours each week in school. It is like your second home. School can be a fun place, but with so many students, furniture and electrical gadgets around, you should be careful and keep yourself (and your friends) safe.

Look at these pairs of pictures. Each pair is about the same action, but the actions are differently done! What are the differences?

1.

2.

3.

Now, talk about these eight actions with your class. Which actions are safe? Why?

Travelling by Train

A train ticket has a lot of information. Look at this train ticket and answer the questions.

1. How many passengers are travelling? ______

11. What is the PNR number of this ticket? ______________

10. What is the destination of this train? ______

9. What is the time of arrival of this train? ______

8. Where is this train leaving from? ______________

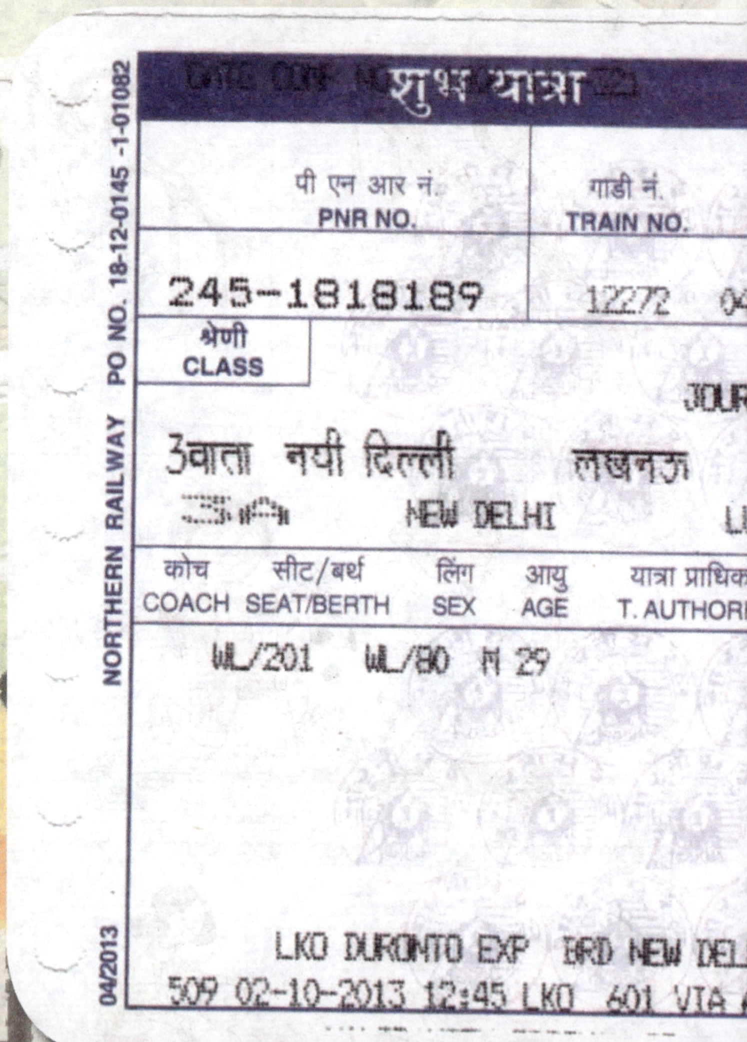

NORTHERN RAILWAY PO NO. 18-12-0145 -1-01082

शुभ यात्रा

पी एन आर नं. PNR NO.	गाडी नं. TRAIN NO.
245-1818189	12272 04

श्रेणी CLASS

JOUR

3वाता नयी दिल्ली लखनऊ

3A NEW DELHI L

कोच COACH	सीट/बर्थ SEAT/BERTH	लिंग SEX	आयु AGE	यात्रा प्राधिक T. AUTHORI
WL/201	WL/80	M	29	

LKO DURONTO EXP BRD NEW DEL

509 02-10-2013 12:45 LKO 601 VIA

04/2013

COOL FACT Indian Railways has a very cute mascot called 'Bholu the Elephant'. He wears the station-master's uniform, and carries a lantern.

2. By what class are they travelling?

 ______

3. Is the ticket confirmed?

 ______

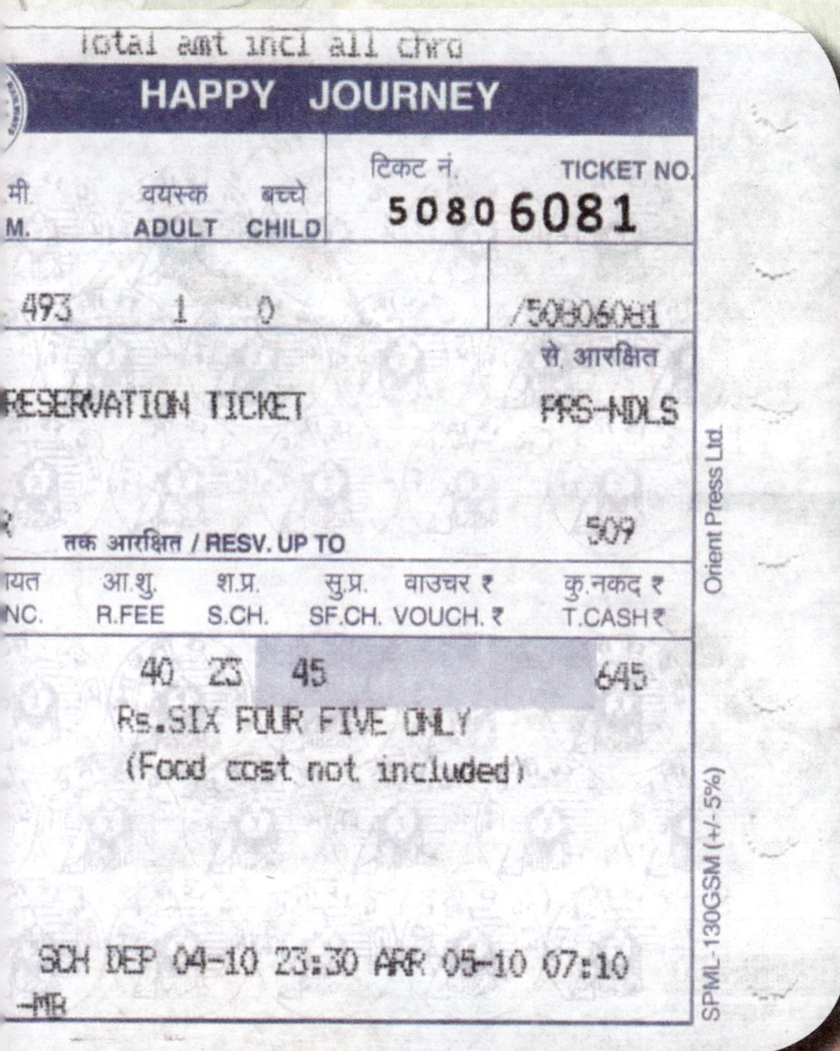

Total amt incl all chrg

HAPPY JOURNEY

मी. M.	वयस्क ADULT	बच्चे CHILD	टिकट नं. TICKET NO. 50806081
493	1	0	/50806081

से. आरक्षित

RESERVATION TICKET PRS-NDLS

तक आरक्षित / RESV. UP TO 509

यत NC.	आ.शु. R.FEE	श.प्र. S.CH.	सु.प्र. SF.CH.	वाउचर ₹ VOUCH. ₹	कु.नकद ₹ T.CASH ₹
40	23	45			645

Rs.SIX FOUR FIVE ONLY

(Food cost not included)

SCH DEP 04-10 23:30 ARR 05-10 07:10

-MB

Orient Press Ltd.

SPML-130GSM (+/-5%)

4. What is the train name?

 ______

5. What is the train number?

 ______

6. What is the time of booking the ticket?

 ______

7. What is the time of departure of this train?

 ______

22

Water Sports and Activities

A. *Swimming, diving and boating are some common water sports. Look at their pictures. Use the given letters as clues and find the names of the water sports in the word search. Then write the full names below the pictures.*

R _ _ _ _ _ G

S _ _ _ _ D _ _ _ _ G

W _ _ _ _ _ _ _ _ _ G

C _ _ _ _ _ _ G

W _ _ _ _ S _ _ _ _ G

Y _ _ _ _ _ _ G

K _ _ _ _ _ _ G

W _ _ _ _ P _ _ O

S _ _ _ _ E _ _ _ _ G

H	F	Z	N	Y	O	C	W	X	U	K	D	W	B
A	A	S	U	P	S	R	A	F	T	I	N	G	J
S	G	N	T	W	L	V	T	Q	N	I	E	X	W
C	H	O	C	A	N	O	E	I	N	G	O	R	Y
U	U	R	S	T	E	A	R	F	U	L	A	V	A
B	K	K	U	E	L	F	P	L	A	Y	M	O	C
A	W	E	E	R	G	C	O	N	Z	E	R	U	H
D	T	L	L	S	O	U	L	A	B	Y	R	I	T
I	B	L	N	K	W	Y	O	D	I	T	U	M	I
V	Q	I	L	I	C	K	E	R	O	S	T	E	N
I	I	N	W	I	N	D	S	U	R	F	I	N	G
N	N	G	K	N	Y	M	P	H	E	T	O	M	A
G	T	L	O	G	A	R	I	S	O	N	E	D	T
L	U	B	V	R	K	A	Y	A	K	I	N	G	G

Let's have fun...

B. *We have learnt a lot of new sports. Some have very long names, don't they? Make six smaller words from the letters in WINDSURFING. All words must be different and have at least 4 letters each.*

______________________ ______________________

______________________ ______________________

______________________ ______________________

COOL FACT Coracles are round, simple boats made of woven leaves, reeds and grass. You can see these in south India on the Kaveri and Tungabhadra rivers, where tourists enjoy a ride on them.

LANGUAGE AND LITERATURE

23

Word Pyramid

A. *Fill in this word pyramid. Start at the top. Each next word has an extra letter. These are the clues to guess the words.*

1. A word for myself is __________.
2. If I am not out, I am __________.
3. Murder and greed are two examples of __________.
4. I have a good musical voice. I can __________.
5. Scorpions, bees and wasps have a painful __________.
6. Violins, guitars and sitars are __________ instruments.
7. The girl is continuously looking at the picture. She is __________.
8. Hurry up! The film is __________ in 5 minutes!
9. Shocking, unexpected, amazing and __________!

B. *Now, let us do it the other way around. Remove one letter at each step to get a new word.*

1. S P R A I N
2. _ _ _ _ _
3. _ _ _ _
4. _ _ _
5. _ _
6. A

C. *Can you make your own word pyramid? It should have at least 5 words.*

COOL FACT In the ancient world, people used to build huge pyramids for burial of important people. The pyramids of Egypt and Central America are very well known.

Money, Money, Money...

A. *Here are the pictures of some rupee coins and notes. Next to each coin or note, write its value.*

= 1.

= 2.

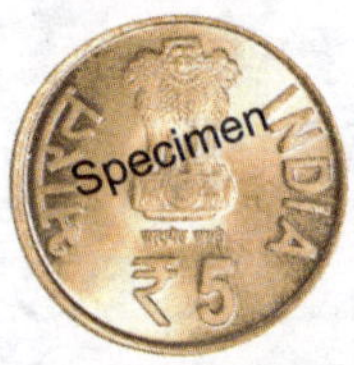

= 3.

= 4.

= 5.

= 6.

= 7.

= 8.

= 9.

= 10.

= 11.

B. *Let us buy things! Write the SMALLEST number of notes and coins needed to buy these six things. The first one has been done for you.*

1. Pencil box: ₹25

   The biggest note that is less than ₹25 is the 20 rupee note. 25-20=5.

   ₹5 can be a note ☐ or a coin ◯. So, the smallest number of notes and coins required here is one note and one coin.

   ☐ 20 + ◯ 5 = 25

Now try these.

2. A cricket bat: ₹2100   ☐ + ☐ = ______

3. Plate of samosas: ₹22   ☐ + ◯ = ______

4. Notebook: ₹32   ☐ + ☐ + ◯ = ______

5. School uniform: ₹555   ☐ + ☐ + ◯ = ______

6. Chocolate bar: ₹16   ☐ + ☐ + ◯ = ______

COOL FACT

Before money was used to buy things, people used animal skins, beads, cattle, blankets and other things as money. They exchanged them for what they needed. This was called the barter system.

LOGICAL REASONING

24

Measures

Complete the paragraph with the correct numbers and measures from the help box.

5 seconds	30 kg	3 hours	250 ml	50 ml
1 minute	1 kg	50 gm	230 km	15 cm

Little Kunal weighs (1.) ________. He travelled (2.) ________ from Delhi to Agra to meet his aunt. In his suitcase, he carried a small bottle of perfume of (3.) ________ and a (4.) ________ box of sweets as gifts for her, some sheets of paper, a pencil and a ruler whose length was (5.) ________ and a (6.) ________ pack of juice. The train journey took almost (7.) ________. His aunt met him at the station with a small bar of chocolate weighing (8.) ________. He ate up the chocolate in the blink of an eye, in just (9.) ________! Once they reached her house, he ran up 3 floors in (10.) ________.

COOL FACT A ruler or a measuring tape has two kinds of units—inches and centimetres. Both can be used to measure length.

25

Animal Families

All animals can be divided into families. Look at the pictures of some animals. Write their names in the correct columns in the table.

Dog family	Cat family	Horse family	Cattle family

COOL FACT

In Rudyard Kipling's famous book *The Jungle Book*, little Mowgli was raised by a pack of wolves. *Raksha* was the she-wolf who took care of Mowgli while *Akela* was the head of the pack.

26

States of North East India

India is a huge country with twenty-nine states and seven Union territories. You can live in India for many, many years without seeing it all.

The North East is connected to the rest of the country through a narrow "neck" of West Bengal. There are eight states: the Seven Sisters and Sikkim.

A. *Look at the map of the North East. Read the sentences about each state, name and colour it using the key within brackets.*

1. **Sikkim:** the "eighth sister", it is like a pinkie finger perched on West Bengal (pink)
2. **Arunachal Pradesh:** The eyebrow over the region and the biggest state. It has a long border with China (green)
3. **Assam:** a state that connects to six other North East states as well as West Bengal (pink)
4. **Mizoram:** the southernmost of the North eastern states (yellow)
5. **Tripura:** a little stub to the west of Mizoram, it shares a border with Bangladesh (green)
6. **Meghalaya:** its name means "abode of the clouds" and it is almost shaped like a cloud (blue)
7. **Nagaland and Manipur:** Nagaland (blue) "sits" over Manipur, they both share a boundary with Myanmar (green)

Cool Activity

Five of India's seven neighbouring countries share a border all around the North East. Now do you know them? Name them!

______________________ ______________________ ______________________

______________________ ______________________

A. *Let us now learn the capitals of these states. In this crossword, the capital cities are missing the vowels a, e, i, o, u. Fill in the vowels and complete the names. The number and names of states are the clues.*

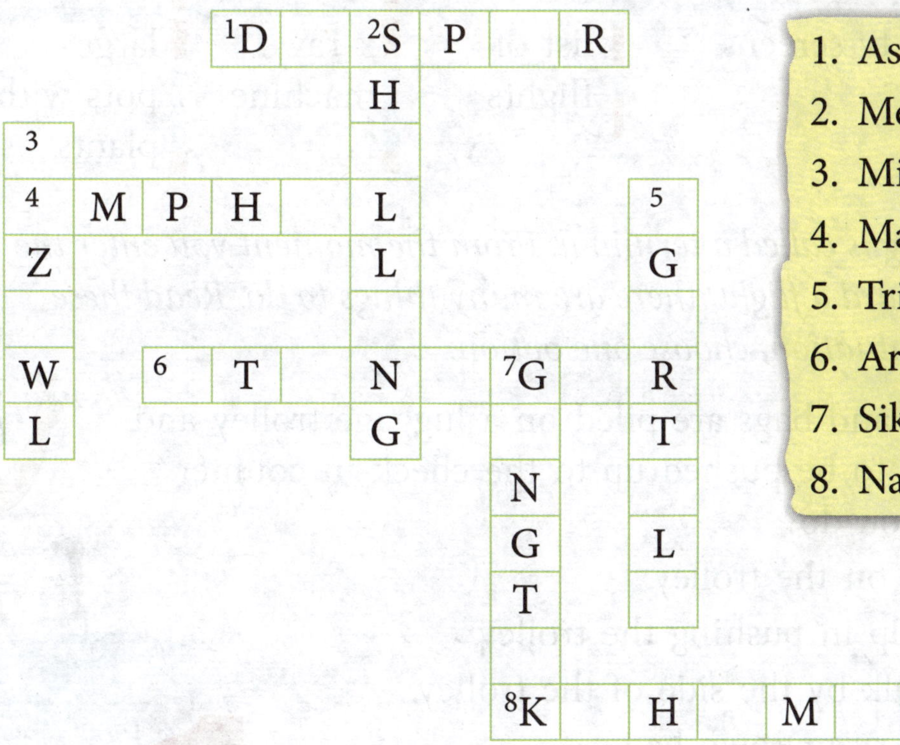

1. Assam
2. Meghalaya
3. Mizoram
4. Manipur
5. Tripura
6. Arunachal Pradesh
7. Sikkim
8. Nagaland

MI

Boarding a Flight

A. *What do you think of when someone says the word 'airport'? Circle the five things that came to your mind first.*

hearing flight announcements	eating a snack at the cafe	pilots	lights on the runway	identity card
pushing a trolley	watching suitcases moving on the luggage belt	tying luggage tags	boarding pass	many aeroplanes
choosing seats	ticket	flight attendants	smooth floor	weighing the suitcase
different uniforms	long queues	buying things in the shops	bookstore	security officers
talking on walkie-talkies	tv screens	list of flights	x-ray machine	large pots with plants

B. *The airport building is called a terminal. From the moment you enter the terminal till you board a flight, there are many things to do. Read these sentences. In each situation, choose one option.*

1. Your suitcases and bags are piled on a luggage trolley and the trolley has to be pushed up to the check-in counter. What would you do?
   a. I would sit on the trolley.
   b. I would help in pushing the trolley.
   c. I would walk by the side of the trolley.
   d. I would carry my own bag.

2. You are at the check-in counter. The airline staff weigh the suitcases and give out tags for carry-on baggage. What would you do?
   a. I would have fun watching the checked-in suitcases sit on the conveyor belt and slowly disappear.
   b. I would read the weight on the screen, count the bags and the tags.
   c. I would tie a tag on each bag.
   d. I would ask the airline staff for a nice seat.

3. Now you have to go through Security Check. What would you do?
   a. I would carry my own boarding pass and get it stamped by the Security Officer.
   b. I would go with my father or mother and help place the hand baggage on the belt for the X-ray machine.
   c. I would count the number of passengers standing in a queue before me.
   d. I would try to look at the X-ray pictures of the things inside each piece of luggage.

4. You have to now go to your boarding gate, but you don't know which gate. What would you do?
   a. I would ask a member of the airline staff or a security guard.
   b. I would look at my boarding pass and try to find the boarding gate.
   c. I would look at the big airport screen and read the list of departures.
   d. I would listen for an announcement regarding my flight.

5. You are now sitting near the correct gate waiting for boarding. You have about half an hour of free time. What would you do?
   a. I would put on my headphones and listen to music.
   b. I would read a book.
   c. I would play with other children or babies who are waiting for the same flight.
   d. I would go take a look at planes taking off and landing.

27

Let's Visit Sri Lanka

Sri Lanka is one of India's neighbours. Read this paragraph about Sri Lanka and fill in the blanks using the help box. But watch out! There are four extra words that do not fit anywhere.

India	national	Strait	Tamil	Republic	Bengali	flag
island	Sinhalese	Dollar	Colombo	kingdom	map	rupee

Sri Lanka is officially called the Democratic Socialist (1.) __________ of Sri Lanka. It is an (2.) __________. It is surrounded by water on all sides. This is the (3.) __________  of Sri Lanka. Its closest neighbour is (4.) __________ , but the two countries are separated by the Palk (5.) __________. The largest city as well as the commercial capital of Sri Lanka is (6.) __________. The currency is the Sri Lankan (7.) __________. The main languages are (8.) __________ and (9.) __________. The (10.) __________ anthem of Sri Lanka is called the Sri Lanka Matha.

COOL FACT

Sri Lanka has many names: ancient Indians called it Lanka or Sinhala, Arab traders called it Serendib and it was officially called Ceylon till 1972.

28

All Creatures Great and Small

A. *Circle the odd ones in the following rows of living creatures.*

1.

2.

3.

B. *Now, match the odd ones with these description clues. In the space given below each clue, write the name of the creature matching it.*

1. It flies at night and sleeps in the day.

   ____

2. It moves very slowly and carries its home on its back.

   ____

3. It lives in water but breathes air.

   ____

4. It looks like an umbrella with many curly legs.

   ____

5. The largest bird, it hides its head in the sand.

   ____

6. A common water bird with webbed feet.

   ____

COOL FACT

All insects have six legs. A spider looks like an insect but has eight legs, so it cannot be called an insect. It spins sticky webs that trap insects and then eats them up.

SCIENCE

29

Looking at the Sky

A. *Look at the picture of the planets and their orbits. Write the names of the planets. Then write 1, 2, 3... to mark the planets from the smallest to the largest. One has been done for you.*

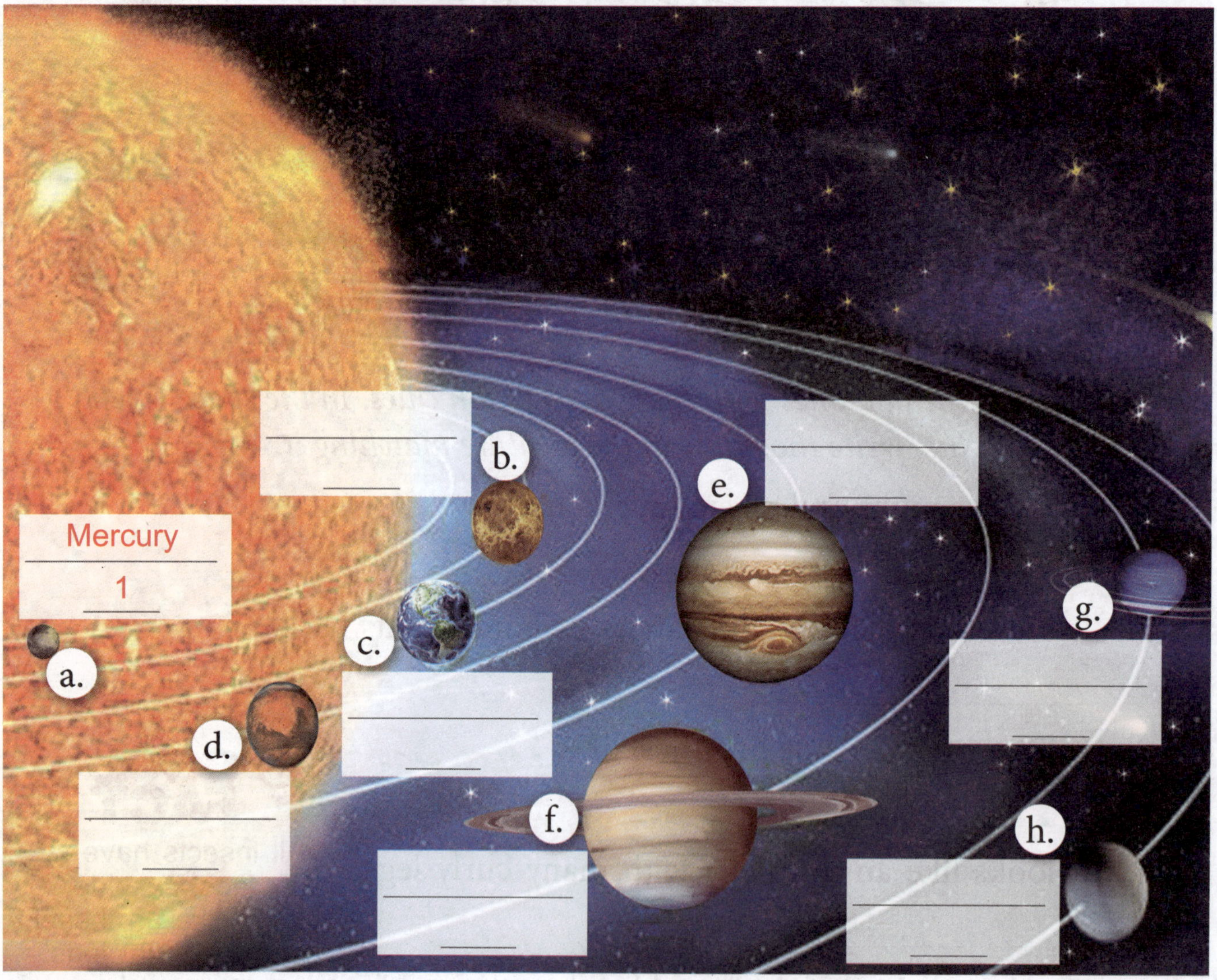

COOL FACT Apart from the Sun, the Moon and the planets, we can see many other objects in the sky. Some of these are clouds, lightning, other stars and comets. Sirius is the brightest star in the night sky. It is also called the Dog Star.

B. *Read the following statements about the heavenly bodies in our solar system and write their names.*

1. What am I?
   a. I am so bright that you cannot see the other objects in the sky during the day.
   b. I am the closest star to the Earth.

2. What am I?
   a. I am not a planet but a satellite. I revolve around the Earth and can be seen at night.
   b. Human beings have landed on my surface.

3. What am I?
   a. I am known as the Morning or Evening Star.
   b. I rotate in a clockwise direction, so for me, the sun rises in the west and sets in the east. Even my day is longer than my year.

4. What am I?
   a. I am popularly known as the red planet and have two small moons called Phobos and Deimos.
   b. India recently launched a space probe called *Mangalyaan* that landed on my surface.

5. What am I?
   a. I am a gassy giant planet with a Great Red Spot on my surface.
   b. I am the largest planet in the solar system, named after the Roman King of Gods.

6. What am I?
   a. I am famous for my rings and can be seen at night even without a telescope.
   b. I am called *Shani* in Indian mythology and a day of the week is named after me.

SCIENCE

30

The Right Key

Look at the following picture of a computer keyboard. Some of the keys do not have symbols. Using the clues, guess the symbols and write them in the blank spaces.

1. Caps Lock - You can use to write in capital letters.
2. Shift - There are two keys like this on the keyboard. If you press this key down together with a letter, you can type the letter in capitals.
3. Enter - There are two keys like this on the keyboard. It helps you to go to the next line or choose an option after marking it.

4. Delete - This key is used to remove any characters typed after the cursor.

5. Backspace - This key is used to remove any characters typed before the cursor.

6. NumLock - If you press this key, the right-hand keypad of numbers gets activated and it is easier to type those number keys.

7. Spacebar - This is the longest key. It allows you to leave space in between your text.

COOL FACT Look at the first 6 letter keys on the keyboard. They read as QWERTY, which is the name given to a standard English language keyboard or keypad (in a phone or tablet).

INDIA

31

India Extremes

India is a land of contrasts. The southernmost parts of the country are in the warm tropics (just eight degrees above the equator), the northernmost and easternmost reaches hug some of the earth's highest mountains, while elsewhere, there is a large and dry desert, some of the world's most fertile plains, the wettest place on earth.

In these three columns, there are labels, pictures, some extra information about the "Extremes". Using the help box, fill in the missing boxes.

1. 	Mount K2 (also called Godwin-Austen)	______ ______ ______
2. 	______ ______ ______	It is in Jammu & Kashmir
3. 	Himalayas	______ ______ ______
4. 	______ ______	Jodhpur, Bikaner and Jaisalmer are cities found in this dry region

5.  Coldest place	Dras	______
6. Hottest place 	Phalodi, in Rajasthan	A temperature of +51 degrees Celsius has been recorded here.
7. 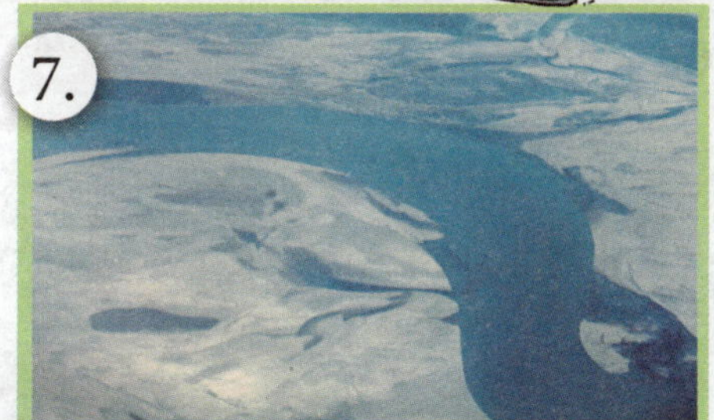	Sunderbans	______
8.  Lowest place in India	Kuttanad, Kerala	The land is upto 3 metres below sea level!
9. 	______	Called the Tsangpo in China.

Brahmaputra
Royal Bengal Tiger's home
8,611 m above sea level
Thar Desert
Temp –45 degrees Celsius
Lake Wular
The world's highest mountain peaks

COOL FACT

The oldest fold mountains and youngest fold mountains in India are the Aravalis and Himalayas respectively. Interestingly, Rashtrapati Bhavan, the Residence of the President of India, is located on Raisina Hill, at the tail end of the Aravali Mountain Range.

LOGICAL REASONING

32

A Twist in Time

Choose words from the help box to replace the underlined words. Watch out, there are two incorrect answers in the box too!

1. Every evening, I play for 3600 seconds.
2. The courier will take 1440 minutes to reach Mumbai.
3. The ship will take 168 hours to reach the next port.
4. The examination is held at the end of a semester.
5. If today is your birthday, you will celebrate it next in 52 weeks' time.
6. We have lived in this house for one decade.
7. Rabindranath Tagore won the Nobel Prize for Literature just over a century ago.
8. The beautiful Brihadishwara Temple in Thanjavur, Tamil Nadu, celebrated one millennium in 2010.

Brihadishwara temple

100 years	1 week	3 months	1 day	1000 years
1000 hours	6 months	10 years	1 hour	1 year

COOL FACT

The moon takes 28 days to revolve around the Earth. It starts with New Moon (when there is no moon at all), takes 14 days to Full Moon and then another 14 days to the next New Moon. The first half is called waxing and the second half is called waning. Each half is called a fortnight.

Quiz Yourself 1

1. Which popular cartoon character had a pet dinosaur called Dino?
2. Which eminent political and social leader is known as the 'Grand Old Man of India'?
3. 'Sorry' and 'Please' are what kind of words—magic or exclamatory?
4. A convertible car has either a soft roof made of canvas or a hard roof made of metal. True or False?
5. Fill in the blank. An ____________ is a freestanding upright support used by an artist to hold the canvas.
6. A carrot is a vegetable. True or false?
7. Which popular tile-matching puzzle game was designed by Alexey Pajitnov?
8. Complete the simile: as ____________ as grass.
9. Which instrument is used to measure the speed of a car?
10. Canberra is the capital city of which country?
11. What is the sound that an owl makes?
12. What kind of pedestrian crossing is named after an animal because of how it looks?
13. There are four athletes in a relay team. True or false?
14. Which beautiful temple in Tamil Nadu was built by the Emperor Raja Chola I one millennium ago?
15. A rebus is a puzzle in which we have to fit together many pieces with interlocking edges to make up a whole picture. True or false?

Quiz Yourself 2

1. How many legs does a spider have?
2. Before money was invented, people used to exchange goods or services in return for other goods or services. What was this system called?
3. Which waterway separates India and Sri Lanka?
4. Which plant has large leaves that are traditionally used as plates for serving food in India?
5. Who composed the national anthem of Bangladesh?

6. Which famous children's book has two wolves named Raksha and Akela?

7. Which is the longest key on a computer keyboard?
8. Who was called the 'Lady with the Lamp'?
9. Which planet comes in between Venus and Mars?
10. Pumpkin is a shrub. True or false?
11. Bholu is the mascot of the Indian Railways. What kind of animal is he?
12. India got its independence in the month of ______________.
13. What are the small, round, lightweight boats used to ferry tourists on Kaveri and Tungabhadra rivers in South India called?
14. Sirius, also known as the ______________ ______________, is the brightest star in the night sky.
15. In which activity does a diver need to wear a 'self-contained underwater breathing apparatus' to breathe underwater?

Keys

Page 9: 1. square; 2. rectangle; 3. rhombus; 4. oblong; 5. parallelogram; 6. trapezium

Page 10-11: A. Magic words sorry, please, thank you, excuse me; Exclamatory words Wow! Hey! Yay! Hurrah! Words of greeting Hi! Good evening! Goodnight! Goodbye! B. 1. a; 2. a; 3. b; 4. b

Page 12: A. 1. carrot; 2. strawberry; 3. apple; 4. pear; 5. pumpkin; 6. apricot; 7. cabbage; 8. turnip; 9. celery; 10. grape; 11. potato; 12. orange B. 1. apples, bananas, grapes, mangoes, water melon, pineapple; 2. radish, tomato, cauliflower, potato, bitter gourd, brinjal, mushroom, lady's finger and apple gourd.

Page 13: A. All the children will get two yellow apples, two red apples and two green apples. B. 1. 2; 2. 4; 3. 2 bananas

Page 16-17: a. 3; b. 2, 2; c. 1, 1, 3; d. 2, 2; e. 2, 2; f. 1, 2

Page 18: Across 1. Snakes and Ladders; 5. Chess; 6. Battleship; 8. Monopoly; Down 1. Scrabble; 2. Ludo; 3. Chinese Checkers; 4. Pictionary; 5. Carrom; 7. Uno

Page 19: A. 1. b; 2. g; 3. a; 4. h; 5. c; 6. i; 7. d; 8. f; 9. e; 10. j B. 4;

Page 20-21: A. 1. steering wheel; 2. speedometer; 3. rear-view mirror; 4. dashboard; 5. fuel indicator; 6. seat belt; 7. wiper; 8. brake; 9. accelerator; 10. headlights; 11. boot; 12. glove compartment

Page 22-23: a. 2; b. 4; c. 6; d. 7; e. 8; f. 9; g. 3; h. 5; i. 10; j. 1

Page 24: 1. Snowy; 2. Hedwig; 3. Mouse; 4. Dinah; 5. Dino

Page 26-27: 1. fire engine; 2. ambulance; 3. police car; 4. bulldozer; 5. mail van; 6. crane; 7. goods train

Page 28-29: 1. 5 dots; 2. 5 toffees; 3. a, B, c; 4. Left fish with 5 scales and right fish with 4 scales; 5. circle, triangle and square; 6. u v w; 7. white square, 8. N o, P q; 9. efg, hij; 10. 3 5, 5 7; 11. 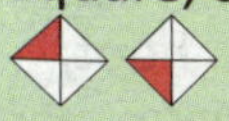 ; 12. 4 6 8, 8 12 16

Page 30: 1. Mahatma Gandhi; 2. Dadabhai Naoroji; 3. Sardar Vallababhai Patel; 4. Sarojini Naidu; 5. Lala Lajpat Rai

Page 31: A. 1. mana; 2. vidhata; 3. Gujarat; 4. Dravida; 5. Yamuna; 6. jage; 7. mage; 8 gatha; 9. mangala; 10. bhagya B. 1. F; 2. T; 3. F

Page 32-33: Trees banyan, orange, apple, mango, coconut, neem; Shrubs jasmine, lemon, hibiscus, rose; Climbers money plant, bougainvillea, pumpkin, grapes, beans; Herbs holy basil, oregano, mint, fenugreek, coriander

Page 34-35: A. 1. ice cream (given); 2. bookworm; 3. pancake; 4. coconut; 5. raincoat; 6. Teapot B. 1. Amsterdam (given) 2. Sydney 3. Moscow 4. Hongkong 5. Rome C. 1. Boston Tea Party 2. Treasure Island 3. Quit India Movement 4. Harry Potter 5. Gold Rush

Page 36: A. 1. b; 2. i; 3. f; 4. c; 5. e; 6. j; 7. a; 8. g; 9. h; 10. d B. Running events a, c, j; Jumping events c, g, h, i; Throwing events b, d, e, f; hurdles is a running and a jumping event.

Page 37: 1. b; 2. a; 3. b; 4. a; 5. a; 6. b

Page 38-39: A. 1. d; 2. e; 3. c; 4. a; 5. g; 6. h; 7. b; 8. f B. 1. Possum; 2. Koala; 3. Kangaroo; 4. Tasmanian Devil

Page 40-41: 1. e; 2. m; 3. d; 4. l; 5. b; 6. g; 7. h; 8. j; 9. i; 10. f; 11. k; 12. c; 13. n; 14. a; 15. o

Page 42-43: 1. 4 p.m. (given); 2. 7:15 p.m.; 3. 6:50 p.m.; 4. 10:30 a.m.; 5. 12:50 p.m.; 6. 6:20 p.m.; 7. 3:30 p.m.; 8. 8:10 a.m.

Page 44-45: 1. Squirrel 2. Basketball; 3. lizard 4. backpack 5. mosquitoes 6. map 7. Compass 8. Torch 9. selfie stick 10. woodpecker 11. tent 12. lantern; 13. campfire 14. butterflies 15. first aid kit; 16. guitar 17. Rope 18. Butterfly net 19. river pebbles 20. Boat 21. chameleon 22. River 23. praying mantis 24. snake

Page 46-47: A. 1. Silver (given); 2. silver 3. bronze; 4. gold; 5. bronze; 6. bronze; 7. bronze; 8. bronze B. 1. badminton 2. wrestling 3. wrestling 4. shooting 5. shooting 6. boxing

Page 48-49: Things that we can eat (edible) strawberry, corn, mustard, pineapple, rice, sugarcane, groundnut, wheat; Things that we cannot eat (inedible) paper, coir mat, jasmine perfume, aloe vera gel, rubber, gunny bag, lemongrass oil, cott on dress, pencil, broom

Page 50: 1. February; 2. April; 3. January; 4. September; 5. March; 6. October; 7. November; 8. May; 9. August; 10. July; 11. December; 12. June

Page 51: 1. torch; 2. sunlight; 3. floodlights; 4. fire; 5. candle; 6. diyas; 7. LASER; 8. LED bulb

Page 52-53: 1. a; 2. b; 3. b; 4. a; 5. a; 6. a; 7. b; 8. a

Page 54-55: 1. d; 2. g; 3. b; 4. f; 5. a; 6. e; 7. c; 8. n; 9. l; 10. i; 11. k; 12. h; 13. m; 14. j

Page 56: 1. Wait for people to get down from a bus or train; 2. Do not play on the road; 3. Walk on the footpath wherever possible; 4. Cross only at a zebra crossing; 5. Hold an adult's hand while crossing the road; 6. Always walk in a direction so that you face traffi c; 7. Use footbridges and subways wherever available; 8. You can cross when the green man lights up

Page 57: 1. Jetpack Joyride 2. Angry Birds; 3. Subway Surfer; 4. Where's my Water; 5. Cut the Rope; 6. Fruit Ninja; 7. Temple Run; 8. Candy Crush Saga;

Page 58-59: 1. Opening an umbrella indoors/ outdoors 2. hiding behind the water cooler/chair 3. handing scissors with the sharp side/handle side 4. Carrying an overloaded/a correctly loaded bag 5. running/walking in the corridor 6. sliding down the banister/walking down stairs 7. playing in the field (while eating) 8. jumping into the pool with/without instructor

Page 60-61: 1. 1; 2. 3 A; 3. no, it is waitlisted; 4. Duronto Express; 5. 12272; 6. 12.45; 7. 23.30; 8. New Delhi; 9. 07.10; 10. Lucknow; 11. 245-1818189

Page 62-63:

H	F	Z	N	Y	O	C	W	X	U	K	D	W	B
A	A	S	U	P	S	R	A	F	T	I	N	G	J
S	G	N	T	W	L	V	T	Q	N	I	E	X	W
C	H	O	C	A	N	O	E	I	N	G	O	R	Y
U	U	R	S	T	E	A	R	F	U	L	A	V	A
B	K	K	U	E	L	F	P	L	A	Y	M	O	C
A	W	E	E	R	G	C	O	N	Z	E	R	U	H
D	T	L	L	S	O	U	L	A	B	Y	R	I	T
I	B	L	N	K	W	Y	O	D	I	T	U	M	I
V	Q	I	L	I	C	K	E	R	O	S	T	E	N
I	I	N	W	I	N	D	S	U	R	F	I	N	G
N	N	G	K	N	Y	M	P	H	E	T	O	M	A
G	T	L	O	G	A	R	I	S	O	N	E	D	T
L	U	B	V	R	K	A	Y	A	K	I	N	G	G

Page 64-65: A. 1. I; 2. in; 3. sin; 4. sing; 5. sting; 6. string; 7. staring; 8. starting; 9. startling B. 1. sprain; 2. Spain; 3. span; 4. pan; 5. an; 6. a

Page 66-67: A. 1. 1; 2. 2; 3. 5; 4. 10; 5. 50; 6. 5; 7. 100; 8. 10; 9. 500; 10. 20; 11. 2000 B. 1. 20+5= 25 (given); 2. 2000+100=2100; 3. 20+2=22; 4. 20+10+2=32; 5. 500+50+5=555; 6. 10+5+1=16

Page 68: 1. 30 kg; 2. 200 km; 3. 50 ml; 4. 1 kg; 5. 15 cm; 6. 250 ml; 7. 3 hours; 8. 50 gm; 9. 5 seconds; 10. 1 minute

Page 69: Dog family d, f, j; Cat family a, g, i; Horse family c, h, l; Cattle family b, e, k

Page 70-71: A.

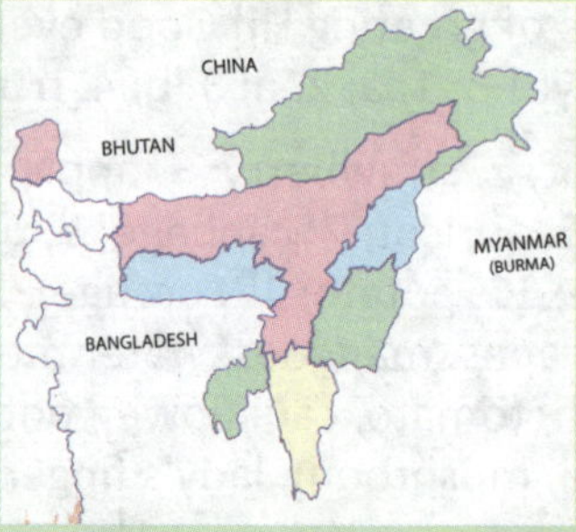

B. 1. Dispur 2. Shillong 3. Aizawl 4. Imphal 5. Agartala 6. Itanagar 7. Gangtok 8. Kohima Cool Activity: Nepal, China, Bhutan, Myanmar (Burma), Bangladesh

Page 74: 1. Republic; 2. island; 3. flag; 4. India; 5. Strait; 6. Colombo; 7. rupee; 8. Sinhalese; 9. Tamil; 10. national

Page 75: A. 1. b and f; 2. d and f; 3. c and f B. 1. bat; 2. snail; 3. dolphin; 4. jelly fish; 5. ostrich; 6. duck

Page 76-77: A. a. Mercury, 1 (given); b. Venus, 3; c. Earth, 4; d. Mars, 2; e. Jupiter, 8; f. Saturn, 7; g. Uranus, 6; h. Neptune, 5 B. 1. sun; 2. Moon; 3. Venus; 4. Mars; 5. Jupiter 6. Saturn

Page 78-79: a. 1. caps lock; b. 2. shift ; c. 7. spacebar; d. 5. back space; e. 6. num lock; f. 3. enter; g. 4. delete; h. 2. shift

Page 80-81: 1. 8611 m. above sea level 2. Lake Wular 3. The world's highest mountain peaks 4. Thar Desert 5. Temp -45°C 6. (answer given) 7. Royal Bengal Tiger's home 8. (answer given) 9. Brahmaputra

Page 82: 1. 1 hour; 2. 1 day; 3. 1 week; 4. 6 months; 5. 1 year; 6. 10 years; 7. 100 years; 8. 1000 years

Page 83: 1. Fred Flintstone; 2. Dadabhai Naoroji; 3. magic words; 4. true; 5. easel; 6. true; 7. Tetris; 8. green; 9. speedometer; 10. Australia; 11. hoot; 12. zebra crossing; 13. true; 14. Brihadishwara Temple; 15. false

Page 84: 1. 8; 2. barter system; 3. Palk Strait; 4. banana; 5. Rabindranath Tagore; 6. The Jungle Book; 7. space bar; 8. Florence Nightingale; 9. Earth; 10. false; 11. elephant; 12. August; 13. coracles; 14. Dog Star; 15. scuba diving